Chemical Facility Security: Issues and Options for the 112th Congress

Dana A. Shea
Specialist in Science and Technology Policy

October 2, 2012

Congressional Research Service

7-5700

www.crs.gov

R41642

CRS Report for Congress ———————————————

Prepared for Members and Committees of Congress

Summary

The Department of Homeland Security (DHS) has statutory authority to regulate chemical facilities for security purposes. The 112th Congress has extended this authority through March 27, 2013. The Obama Administration has requested a one-year extension of this authority until October 4, 2013. Congressional policymakers have debated the scope and details of reauthorization and continue to consider legislation establishing an authority with longer duration. Some Members of Congress support an extension, either short- or long-term, of the existing authority. Other Members call for revision and more extensive codification of chemical facility security regulatory provisions. Questions regarding the current law's effectiveness in reducing chemical facility risk and the sufficiency of federal funding for chemical facility security exacerbate the tension between continuing current policies and changing the statutory authority.

Congressional policymakers have questioned DHS's effectiveness in implementing the authorized regulations, called chemical facility anti-terrorism standards (CFATS). The DHS finalized CFATS regulations in 2007. No chemical facilities have completed the CFATS process, which starts with information submission by chemical facilities and finishes with inspection and approval of facility security measures by DHS. Several factors, including the amount of detailed information provided to DHS, effectiveness of DHS program management, and the availability of CFATS inspectors, likely complicate the inspection process and lead to delays in inspection. Policymakers have questioned whether the compliance rate with CFATS is sufficient to address this homeland security issue.

Key policy issues debated in previous Congresses contribute to the current reauthorization debate. These issues include the adequacy of DHS resources and efforts; the appropriateness and scope of federal preemption of state chemical facility security activities; the availability of information for public comment, potential litigation, and congressional oversight; the range of chemical facilities identified by DHS; and the ability of inherently safer technologies to achieve security goals.

The 112th Congress might take various approaches to this issue. Congress might allow the statutory authority to expire but continue providing appropriations to administer the regulations. Congress might permanently or temporarily extend the statutory authority to observe the impact of the current regulations and, if necessary, address any perceived weaknesses at a later date. Congress might codify the existing regulations in statute and reduce the discretion available to the Secretary of Homeland Security to change the current regulatory framework. Alternatively, Congress might substantively change the current regulation's implementation, scope, or impact by amending the existing statute or creating a new one. Finally, Congress might choose to terminate the program by allowing its authority to lapse and removing funding for the program. This would leave regulation of chemical facility security to state and local governments.

Both appropriation and authorization legislation in the 112th Congress address chemical facility security. P.L. 112-175 extended the existing authority until March 27, 2013. Both FY2013 homeland security appropriations bills (S. 3216 and H.R. 5855, as passed by the House) would extend the existing authority until October 4, 2013. Authorizing legislation includes H.R. 225; H.R. 901, reported as amended by the House Committee on Homeland Security and referred to the House Committee on Energy and Commerce; H.R. 908, reported as amended by the House Committee on Energy and Commerce; H.R. 916; H.R. 2890; S. 473, reported as amended by the Senate Committee on Homeland Security and Governmental Affairs; S. 709; and S. 711.

Contents

Tables

Contacts

Introduction

Even before September 11, 2001, congressional policymakers expressed concern about the safety and security of facilities possessing certain amounts of hazardous chemicals. The sudden release of hazardous chemicals from facilities storing large quantities might potentially harm many people living or working near the facility. Historically, chemical facilities engaged in security activities on a voluntary basis. Following September 11, 2001, some states enacted laws requiring additional consideration of security at chemical facilities.[1] Congress debated whether the federal government should reduce the risk such facilities pose by regulating them for security purposes. In 2006, the 109th Congress passed legislation providing the Department of Homeland Security (DHS) with statutory authority to regulate chemical facilities for security purposes. Subsequent Congresses have extended this authority. This statutory authority expires on March 27, 2013. The Obama Administration has requested a one-year extension of this authority until October 4, 2013.[2] Both FY2013 homeland security appropriations bills (S. 3216 and H.R. 5855) would extend the existing authority until October 4, 2013. Advocacy groups, stakeholders, and policymakers have called for congressional reauthorization of this authority, though they disagree about the preferred approach. Congress may extend the existing authority, revise the existing authority to resolve potentially contentious issues, or allow this authority to lapse.

This report provides a brief overview of the existing statutory authority and implementing regulation. It describes several policy issues raised in previous debates regarding chemical facility security and identifies policy options for congressional consideration. Finally, it discusses legislation in the 112th Congress.

Overview of Statute and Regulation

The 109th Congress provided DHS with statutory authority to regulate chemical facilities for security purposes.[3] The statute explicitly identified some DHS authorities and left other aspects to the discretion of the Secretary of Homeland Security. The statute contains a "sunset provision" and expires on October 4, 2012.[4] The Obama Administration has requested a one-year extension of this authority until October 4, 2013.[5]

---

[1] For example, New Jersey, Maryland, and New York each enacted laws addressing security at chemical facilities.

[2] Office of Management and Budget, The White House, *Budget of the United States Government, Fiscal Year 2013, Appendix*, p. 597.

[3] Section 550, P.L. 109-295, Department of Homeland Security Appropriations Act, 2007.

[4] The original statute expired on October 4, 2009, three years after enactment. The Department of Homeland Security Appropriations Act, 2010 (P.L. 111-83) extended the existing statutory authority an additional year. The Continuing Appropriations Act, 2011 (P.L. 111-242) extended the statutory authority through December 3, 2010. The second continuing resolution (P.L. 111-290) extended the statutory authority through December 18, 2010. The third continuing resolution (P.L. 111-317) extended the statutory authority through December 21, 2010. The Continuing Appropriations and Surface Transportation Extensions Act, 2011 (P.L. 111-322) extended the statutory authority through March 4, 2011. The Further Continuing Appropriations Amendments, 2011 (P.L. 112-4) extended the statutory authority through March 18, 2011. The Additional Continuing Appropriations Amendments, 2011 (P.L. 112-6) extended the statutory authority through April 8, 2011. The Further Additional Continuing Appropriations Amendments, 2011 (P.L. 112-8) extended the statutory authority through April 15, 2011. The Department of Defense and Full-Year Continuing Appropriations Act, 2011 (P.L. 112-10) and the Continuing Appropriations Act, 2012 (P.L. 112-33) both extended the statutory authority through October 4, 2011. The Continuing Appropriations Act, 2012 (P.L. 112-36) extended the statutory authority through November 18, 2011. The Consolidated and Further Continuing Appropriations Act, 2012, (continued...)

On April 9, 2007, the Department of Homeland Security issued an interim final rule regarding the chemical facility anti-terrorism standards (CFATS).[6] This interim final rule entered into force on June 8, 2007. The interim final rule implements both statutory authority explicit in P.L. 109-295, Section 550, and authorities DHS found Congress implicitly granted. In promulgating the interim final rule, DHS interpreted the language of the statute to determine what DHS asserts was the intent of Congress. Consequently, much of the rule arises from the Secretary's discretion and interpretation of legislative intent rather than explicit statutory language.

Under the interim final rule, the Secretary of Homeland Security determines which chemical facilities must meet regulatory security requirements, based on the degree of risk posed by each facility. The DHS lists 322 chemicals as "chemicals of interest" for the purposes of compliance with CFATS.[7] The DHS considers each chemical in the context of three threats: release; theft or diversion; and sabotage and contamination. Chemical facilities with greater than specified quantities of potentially dangerous chemicals must submit information to DHS, so that DHS can determine the facility's risk status. The statute exempts several types of facilities from this requirement: facilities defined as a water system or wastewater treatment works; facilities owned or operated by the Department of Defense or Department of Energy; facilities regulated by the Nuclear Regulatory Commission; and those facilities regulated under the Maritime Transportation Security Act of 2002 (P.L. 107-295).

Based on the submitted information, DHS determines the risk associated with each facility. Facilities DHS deems high risk must meet CFATS requirements. The DHS assigns high-risk facilities into one of four risk-based tiers. Facilities in higher risk tiers must meet more stringent performance-based requirements. The statute mandated the use of performance-based security requirements.[8] The DHS created graduated performance-based requirements for facilities assigned to each risk-based tier.

(...continued)

(P.L. 112-55) extended the statutory authority through December 16, 2011. P.L. 112-67 extended the statutory authority through December 17, 2011. P.L. 112-68 extended the statutory authority through December 23, 2011. The Consolidated Appropriations Act, 2012 (P.L. 112-74) extended the statutory authority through October 4, 2012. The Continuing Appropriations Resolution, 2013 (P.L. 112-175) extends the statutory authority through March 27, 2013.

[5] Office of Management and Budget, The White House, *Budget of the United States Government, Fiscal Year 2013, Appendix*, p. 597.

[6] 72 *Federal Register* 17688-17745 (April 9, 2007). An interim final rule is a rule that meets the requirements for a final rule and that has the same force and effect as a final rule, but contains an invitation for further public comment on its provisions. After reviewing comments to the interim final rule, an agency may modify the interim final rule and issue a "final" final rule. The DHS first issued the proposed rule in December 2006 and solicited public comments. 71 *Federal Register* 78276-78332 (December 28, 2006).

[7] 72 *Federal Register* 65396-65435 (November 20, 2007).

[8] According to the White House Office of Management and Budget, a performance standard is a standard

> that states requirements in terms of required results with criteria for verifying compliance but without stating the methods for achieving required results. A performance standard may define the functional requirements for the item, operational requirements, and/or interface and interchangeability characteristics. A performance standard may be viewed in juxtaposition to a prescriptive standard which may specify design requirements, such as materials to be used, how a requirement is to be achieved, or how an item is to be fabricated or constructed.

For example, a performance standard might require that a facility perimeter be secured. In contrast, a prescriptive standard might dictate the height and type of fence to be used to secure the perimeter. See Office of Management and Budget, The White House, "Federal Participation in the Development and Use of Voluntary Consensus Standards and in Conformity Assessment Activities," *Circular A-119*, February 10, 1998.

All high-risk facilities must assess their vulnerabilities, develop an effective security plan, submit these documents to DHS, and implement their security plan.[9] The vulnerability assessment serves two purposes under the interim final rule. One is to determine or confirm the placement of the facility in a risk-based tier. The other is to provide a baseline against which to evaluate the site security plan activities.

The site security plans must address the vulnerability assessment by describing how activities in the plan correspond to securing facility vulnerabilities. Additionally, the site security plan must address preparations for and deterrents against specific modes of potential terrorist attack, as applicable and identified by DHS. The site security plans must also describe how the activities taken by the facility meet the risk-based performance standards provided by DHS.

The DHS must review and approve the submitted documents, audit and inspect chemical facilities, and determine regulatory compliance. The DHS may disapprove submitted vulnerability assessments or site security plans that fail to meet DHS performance-based standards, but not because of the presence or absence of a specific security measure. In the case of disapproval, DHS must identify in writing those areas of the assessment and/or plan that need improvement. Owners or operators of chemical facilities may appeal such decisions to DHS.

Similarly, if, after inspecting a chemical facility, DHS finds the facility not in compliance, the Secretary must write to the facility explaining the deficiencies found, provide an opportunity for the facility to consult with DHS, and issue an order to the facility to comply by a specified date. If the facility continues to be out of compliance, DHS may fine and, eventually, order the facility to cease operation. The interim final rule establishes the process by which chemical facilities can appeal DHS decisions and rulings, but the statute prohibits third-party suits for enforcement purposes.

The statute requires certain protections for information developed in compliance with this act. The interim final rule creates a category of information exempted from disclosure under the Freedom of Information Act (FOIA) and comparable state and local laws. The DHS named this category of information "Chemical-terrorism Vulnerability Information" (CVI). Information generated under the interim final rule, as well as any information developed for chemical facility security purposes identified by the Secretary, comprise this category. Judicial and administrative proceedings shall treat CVI as classified information. The DHS asserts sole discretion regarding who will be eligible to receive CVI. Disclosure of CVI may be punishable by fine.

The interim final rule states it preempts state and local regulation that "conflicts with, hinders, poses an obstacle to, or frustrates the purposes of" the federal regulation. States, localities, or affected companies may request a decision from DHS regarding potential conflict between the regulations. Since DHS promulgated the interim final rule, Congress amended P.L. 109-295, Section 550, to state that such preemption will occur only in the case of an "actual conflict."[10] The DHS has not issued revised regulations addressing this change in statute.

---

[9] High-risk facilities may develop vulnerability assessments and site security plans using alternative security programs so long as they meet the tiered, performance-based requirements of the interim final rule.

[10] Section 534, P.L. 110-161, the Consolidated Appropriations Act, 2008.

Implementation

Within DHS, the National Protection and Programs Directorate (NPPD) is responsible for chemical facility security regulations. Within NPPD, the Office of Infrastructure Protection, through its Infrastructure Security Compliance Division (ISCD), oversees the CFATS program.[11] This section reviews implementation of the chemical facility security regulations, focusing on funding, the number of regulated facilities, rate of facility inspection, and DHS's internal review of its implementation efforts.

Appropriated Funding and Staff

As seen in **Table 1**, requested and appropriated funding for this program generally increased since its creation, but decreased since FY2011. Full-time equivalent staffing for this program has also increased over time. This increase in staffing reflects, in part, the development of a cadre of CFATS inspectors, based in regional offices.

The DHS received statutory authority to regulate chemical facilities in 2006. It did not possess a chemical facility security office or inspector cadre at that time. The DHS requested additional positions to create an inspector cadre. As of February 2012, DHS had hired 102 of a planned 108 inspectors and all of 14 field leadership positions.[12] Chemical inspectors must be able to assess the security measures at a chemical facility using the performance-based criteria developed by DHS. Performance-based security measures are likely more difficult than prescriptive measures for chemical inspectors to assess and thus may require greater training and experience in the inspector cadre. To overcome this challenge, DHS has established a Basic Inspector School training program. Such training, while likely improving the quality of inspection, also introduces additional time between the hiring of new inspectors and their deployment in the field.

For FY2013, the House of Representatives and the Senate Committee on Appropriations have recommended different funding levels. The House would appropriate $45 million, a decrease of $30 million from the FY2013 request and $48 million from the FY2012 appropriation. In addition, the House report states, "in spite of ample appropriations provided by Congress, the Department has made little progress carrying out its regulatory responsibilities for ... the Chemical Facility Anti-Terrorism Standards (CFATS) program...."[13] The Senate committee, in contrast, recommends $86 million, an increase of $11 million from the FY2013 request and a decrease of $7 million from the FY2012 appropriation. The Senate committee states, "it would be shortsighted, in the meantime, to take the full amount of [Administration's] proposed savings when the need for improvement has been documented. Funding will not resolve all of the outstanding issues, but the proposed cuts are too deep to ensure change for the better can be

---

[11] The budget request for the Infrastructure Security Compliance Project contains the funding and personnel allocations for implementing the CFATS regulations.

[12] Testimony of Rand Beers, Under Secretary, National Protection and Programs Directorate, Department of Homeland Security, before the House Committee on Energy and Commerce, Subcommittee on Environment and the Economy, February 3, 2012. The DHS has increased the hired number of inspectors. In July 2010, DHS had hired 88 field personnel, including 11 regional commanders. Office of Infrastructure Protection, National Protection and Programs Directorate, Department of Homeland Security, *Update on Implementation of the Chemical Facility Anti-Terrorism Standards and Development of Ammonium Nitrate Regulations-2010 Chemical Sector Coordinating Council Security Summit*, July 7, 2010.

[13] H.Rept. 112-492, accompanying H.R. 5855, Department of Homeland Security Appropriations Bill, 2013, p. 101.

---

completed."[14] The Senate report also would direct DHS to retain an inspector cadre of no fewer than 148 FTE for FY2013.

Table 1. DHS Funding for Chemical Facility Security Regulation by Fiscal Year

Fiscal Year	Request ($ in millions)	Appropriation ($ in millions)	Full-time Equivalents
FY2007	10	22[a]	0
FY2008	25	50	21
FY2009	63	78[b]	78
FY2010	103[c]	103[d]	246
FY2011	105[e]	96[e]	257
FY2012	99[e]	93[e]	242
FY2013	75[f]		242

Source: Department of Homeland Security, Preparedness Directorate, Infrastructure Protection and Information Security, *FY2007 Congressional Justification*; Department of Homeland Security, National Protection and Programs Directorate, Infrastructure Protection and Information Security, *Fiscal Year 2008 Congressional Justification*; Department of Homeland Security, National Protection and Programs Directorate, Infrastructure Protection and Information Security, *Fiscal Year 2009 Congressional Justification*; Department of Homeland Security, National Protection and Programs Directorate, Infrastructure Protection and Information Security, *Fiscal Year 2010 Congressional Justification*; Department of Homeland Security, National Protection and Programs Directorate, Infrastructure Protection and Information Security, *Fiscal Year 2011 Overview Congressional Justification*; Department of Homeland Security, National Protection and Programs Directorate, Infrastructure Protection and Information Security, *Fiscal Year 2012 Congressional Justification*; Department of Homeland Security, National Protection and Programs Directorate, Infrastructure Protection and Information Security, *Fiscal Year 2013 Congressional Justification*; H.Rept. 109-699; P.L. 110-28; the explanatory statement for P.L. 110-161 at *Congressional Record*, December 17, 2007, p. H16092; the explanatory statement for P.L. 110-329 at *Congressional Record*, September 24, 2008, pp. H9806-H9807; H.Rept. 111-298; P.L. 111-242, as amended; S.Rept. 112-74; and H.Rept. 112-331.

Notes: Funding levels rounded to nearest million. A full-time equivalent equals one staff person working a full-time work schedule for one year. The DHS requests funding for chemical facility security through the Infrastructure Security Compliance Project.

a. Includes funds provided in supplemental appropriations (P.L. 110-28).

b. Of this amount appropriated for the Infrastructure Security Compliance Project, $5 million were designated for activities related to the development of ammonium nitrate regulations.

c. Of this amount requested for the Infrastructure Security Compliance Project, $14 million were designated for activities related to the development of ammonium nitrate regulations.

d. Of this amount appropriated for the Infrastructure Security Compliance Project, $14 million were designated for activities related to the development of ammonium nitrate regulations.

e. The DHS planned to use an unspecified amount of these funds to regulate ammonium nitrate sale and transfer.

f. The DHS plans to use an unspecified amount of these requested funds to regulate ammonium nitrate sale and transfer.

The DHS has responded to the House-passed funding level, stating that this level of appropriations would

---

[14] S.Rept. 112-169, accompanying S. 3216, Department of Homeland Security Appropriations Bill, 2013, p. 98.

drastically curtail DHS's ability to: 1) implement the statutory and regulatory requirements for the security of high-risk chemical facilities as specified in CFATS; 2) continue development of the proposed Ammonium Nitrate Security Program; and 3) fully implement the program improvements identified in the ISCD Action Plan. DHS estimates that, after expending approximately $35 million for salaries and benefits for 242 FTEs, approximately $12 million would remain for implementing CFATS and completing development of the proposed Ammonium Nitrate Security Program. DHS would be forced to cease virtually all activities under CFATS other than those directly related to reviewing SSPs and performing facility inspections—which means those other activities would be significantly delayed. At the proposed $45.4 million funding level, the Department's ability to conduct the most basic CFATS functions would be impacted. These include maintaining the CSAT and the Chemical-Security Management System information technology systems, and acquiring important technical and subject matter support. Additionally, CFATS-related outreach and engagement with the regulated community would be significantly reduced and some aspects would cease....[15]

Number of Regulated Facilities

The DHS has assessed initial information submissions from more than 41,000 chemical facilities. The DHS considered more than 7,800 of these facilities as preliminarily high-risk and required each to submit a site vulnerability assessment. From the submitted site vulnerability assessments, DHS identified and placed 4,433 facilities into preliminary or final risk tiers. **Table 2** shows the number of high-risk facilities in each tier as of July 31, 2012, with Tier 1 those facilities of highest risk.

Table 2. Facilities Regulated by DHS under CFATS

Risk Tier	Facilities with Final Tier Decision	Facilities Awaiting Final Tier Decision	Total Facilities
1	114	7	121
2	454	51	505
3	1,071	170	1,241
4	2,023	535	2,558
Total	**3,662**	**763**	**4,425**

Source: Infrastructure Security Compliance Division, Office of Infrastructure Protection, National Protection and Programs Directorate, Department of Homeland Security, *Chemical Facility Anti-Terrorism Standards (CFATS) and Ammonium Nitrate Security Regulation Update*, July 31, 2012.

Notes: The DHS has preliminarily assigned some facilities to a risk tier. Final assignment to a risk tier occurs after final review of submitted vulnerability assessments. The discrepancy between the total facilities in the table and in the text above is due to slightly different reporting dates.

In May 2010, DHS identified an anomaly in one of the risk-assessment tools used by DHS to determine a facility's risk tier. At that time, DHS believed that it had resolved the anomaly. In June 2011, a new acting ISCD Director "rediscovered" this issue, identified its potential effect on

---

[15] Testimony of Suzanne Spaulding, Deputy Under Secretary, National Protection and Programs Directorate, Department of Homeland Security, before the House Committee on Appropriations, Subcommittee on Homeland Security, July 26, 2012.

facility tiering, brought the issue to the attention of NPPD leadership,[16] and notified facilities of their change in risk tier.[17] Subsequent review of this risk-assessment tool resulted in DHS reassigning approximately 500 facilities to a lower risk tier.[18] The DHS lowered the number of facilities allocated to the highest-risk tier from 211 to 102, a greater than 50% reduction.[19] In some cases, DHS determined that some facilities no longer qualified as a high-risk facility and thus were not subject to CFATS regulation.

Overall, the total number of chemical facilities assigned a risk tier by DHS has declined since the CFATS program began. Several factors may have contributed to this decline, including erroneous filing by regulated entities, process changes on the part of regulated entities, and business operations and decisions. The DHS has also engaged in targeted outreach activities to identify those facilities that fall under the regulation but have not yet complied by filing required information. The DHS asserts that the observed reduction in regulated chemical facilities indicates that the CFATS program and its statutory authority are increasing security by inducing voluntary reductions in chemical holdings by regulated entities.

Facility Inspections

The DHS planned to begin inspections of Tier 1 facilities as quickly as 14 months after issuance of regulations.[20] Several factors have delayed inspections, including the release of additional regulatory information in the form of an appendix and the need to build an inspector cadre, to establish a regional infrastructure, and to perform pre-authorization inspections at facilities. DHS officials have provided a series of timeframes for beginning inspections.[21] The DHS began

---

[16] Oral testimony of Rand Beers, Under Secretary, National Protection and Programs Directorate, Department of Homeland Security, before the House Committee on Energy and Commerce, Subcommittee on Environment and the Economy, February 3, 2012.

[17] Department of Homeland Security, "DHS Notifies Chemical Facilities of Revised Tiering Assignments," July 5, 2011, http://www.dhs.gov/files/programs/cfats-revised-tiering-assignments.shtm.

[18] Society of Chemical Manufacturers and Affiliates, "DHS Provides Latest on CFATS and Tiering at Chemical Sector Security Summit," http://www.socma.com/tags/printerFriendly.cfm?pageid=3109.

[19] CRS analysis of Department of Homeland Security data from Infrastructure Security Compliance Division, Office of Infrastructure Protection, National Protection and Programs Directorate, Department of Homeland Security, *Chemical Facility Anti-Terrorism Standards*, January 27, 2011; Personal communication with Department of Homeland Security, September 15, 2011; and AcuTech Consulting Group, *A Survey of CFATS Progress in Securing the Chemical Sector*, September 6, 2011.

[20] Department of Homeland Security, *Chemical Facility Anti-Terrorism Standards Interim Final Rule Regulatory Assessment*, DHS-2006-0073, April 1, 2007, p. 15.

[21] In July 2007, DHS provided testimony that formal site inspections of a selected group of facilities would begin by the end of the calendar year (Testimony of Robert B. Stephan, Assistant Secretary for Infrastructure Protection, National Protection and Programs Directorate, Department of Homeland Security, before the House Committee on Homeland Security, Subcommittee on Transportation Security and Infrastructure, July 24, 2007). In December 2007, DHS provided testimony that facility inspection would begin in fall of 2008 (Testimony of Robert B. Stephan, Assistant Secretary for Infrastructure Protection, National Protection and Programs Directorate, Department of Homeland Security, before the House Committee on Homeland Security, Subcommittee on Transportation Security and Infrastructure, December 13, 2007). In 2009, DHS provided testimony that inspections would begin in the first quarter of FY2010 (Testimony of Philip Reitinger, Deputy Under Secretary, National Protection and Programs Directorate, Department of Homeland Security, before the House Committee on Homeland Security, June 16, 2009). In 2011, DHS stated that it expected to inspect all Tier 1 facilities by the end of calendar year 2011 (Oral testimony of Rand Beers, Under Secretary, National Protection and Programs Directorate, Department of Homeland Security, before the House Committee on Homeland Security, Subcommittee on Cybersecurity, Infrastructure Protection, and Security Technologies, February 11, 2011).

---

inspections of Tier 1 facilities in February 2010.[22] At that time, DHS testified that it planned to inspect all Tier 1 facilities by the end of calendar year 2010,[23] but DHS had only performed nine authorization inspections as of September 2011.[24] Similarly, although DHS subsequently stated that it expected to inspect all Tier 1 facilities by the end of calendar year 2011,[25] it had approved 10 site security plans and no implementation of any site security plan by that time.[26] Since then, DHS has implemented an interim site security plan review process that it asserts is more effective and timely. The DHS has used this interim review process to authorize additional site security plans. As of September 9, 2012, DHS had approved or conditionally approved 73 site security plans.[27] The DHS also reported that it had successfully inspected and approved the site security plan implementation at two facilities.

The DHS also identifies annual performance measures for the inspection of high-risk chemical facilities. The DHS uses as a performance measure the ratio of inspected high-risk chemical facilities that are compliant with CFATS risk-based performance standards to the number of high-risk chemical facilities selected for inspection each year.[28] **Table 3** summarizes the information presented by DHS in its annual performance reports. While DHS set target goals of high levels of compliance within inspected facilities, DHS did not meet this goal in FY2008. Beginning in FY2011, DHS lowered the target goal. The DHS reports in the most recent annual performance report that 9.1% of inspected chemical facilities were compliant, even though DHS has testified that no chemical facility has had a successful authorization inspection.[29]

---

[22] Testimony of Rand Beers, Under Secretary, National Protection and Programs Directorate, Department of Homeland Security, before the Senate Committee on Homeland Security and Governmental Affairs, March 3, 2010.

[23] Oral testimony of Rand Beers, Under Secretary, National Protection and Programs Directorate, Department of Homeland Security, before the Senate Committee on Homeland Security and Governmental Affairs, March 3, 2010.

[24] Personal communication with Department of Homeland Security, September 15, 2011.

[25] Oral testimony of Rand Beers, Under Secretary, National Protection and Programs Directorate, Department of Homeland Security, before the House Committee on Homeland Security, Subcommittee on Cybersecurity, Infrastructure Protection, and Security Technologies, February 11, 2011.

[26] Personal communication with Department of Homeland Security, January 5, 2012.

[27] Testimony of Rand Beers, Under Secretary, National Protection and Programs Directorate, Department of Homeland Security, before the House Committee on Energy and Commerce, Subcommittee on Environment and the Economy, September 11, 2012. As of July 16, 2012, DHS had approved 63 site security plans (Testimony of Suzanne Spaulding, Deputy Under Secretary, National Protection and Programs Directorate, Department of Homeland Security, before the House Committee on Appropriations, Subcommittee on Homeland Security, July 26, 2012). As of January 23, 2012, DHS had approved 53 site security plans (Testimony of Rand Beers, Under Secretary, National Protection and Programs Directorate, Department of Homeland Security, before the House Committee on Energy and Commerce, Subcommittee on Environment and the Economy, February 3, 2012).

[28] Note that this performance measure does not reflect compliance of high-risk chemical facilities as a whole, but only compliance of those inspected.

[29] As of September 2011, DHS had performed 9 authorization inspections. The DHS issued no inspected facility a letter of authorization, which would indicate that the facility was compliant with CFATS. The DHS temporarily ceased inspections following its internal review but has restarted its authorization inspections. Testimony of Suzanne Spaulding, Deputy Under Secretary, National Protection and Programs Directorate, Department of Homeland Security, before the House Committee on Appropriations, Subcommittee on Homeland Security, July 26, 2012.

Table 3. Reported Percentage of Inspected High-Risk Chemical Facilities in Compliance with CFATS Risk-Based Performance Standards

(Percent Compliance)

Report Year	FY2008		FY2009		FY2010		FY2011		FY2012		FY2013	
	Goal	Actual	Goal	Actual	Goal	Actual	Goal	Actual	Goal	Actual	Goal	Actual
2007	75%	—	75%	—								
2008a	75%	0%	85%	—	70%	—						
2010b							10%	—	20%	—		
2011c							10%	9.1%	20%	—	35%	—

Source: CRS analysis of Department of Homeland Security, *Annual Performance Report: Fiscal Years 2007-2009*, p. 48; Department of Homeland Security, *Annual Performance Report: Fiscal Years 2008-2010*, p. 60; Department of Homeland Security, *Annual Performance Report: Fiscal Years 2010-2012*, p. 9; and Department of Homeland Security, *Annual Performance Report: Fiscal Years 2011-2013*, p. 11.

Notes: The DHS did not issue a performance report for 2009-2011.

a. The DHS notes that "The Chemical Facility Anti-Terrorism Standards regulatory process is not at the point at which inspections can commence. Therefore our planned target of 75 percent was not met. Security Vulnerability Assessments for high-risk facilities are being submitted for review on a timeline that culminates at the end of calendar year 2008. After review of Security Vulnerability Assessments, facilities will be issued a final risk determination and will submit their Site Security Plans in mid-2009. After Site Security Plans are completed, facilities will be inspected for compliance with the risk based performance standards."

b. The DHS notes that "This measures a program that is in its early stages of implementation – targets will continue to increase."

c. The DHS notes that "The deviation from the performance target was slight and attributable to scheduled authorization inspections in September 2011 being postponed due to Hurricane Irene. There was no effect on overall program performance. This program is in the early stages of implementation and targets will continue to increase."

Beyond challenges related to program management, DHS identified an additional factor in the delay of the inspection schedule: the necessary iteration between DHS and the regulated entity regarding its site security plan.[30] The DHS has issued 66 administrative orders to compel facilities to complete their site security plans.[31] In addition, DHS established a pre-authorization inspection process to gain additional information from facilities to fully assess the submitted site security plan. Once DHS completes a pre-authorization inspection at a facility, the facility may amend its site security plan to reflect the results of the pre-authorization inspection. The DHS had performed approximately 180 pre-authorization inspections as of February 2012.[32]

---

[30] The DHS identified such iteration on the contents of site security plans as one factor delaying the start of the inspection process from December 2009 to February 2010. Oral testimony of Rand Beers, Under Secretary, National Protection and Programs Directorate, Department of Homeland Security, before the Senate Committee on Homeland Security and Governmental Affairs, March 3, 2010.

[31] Testimony of Rand Beers, Under Secretary, National Protection and Programs Directorate, Department of Homeland Security, before the House Committee on Energy and Commerce, Subcommittee on Environment and the Economy, March 31, 2011.

[32] Testimony of Rand Beers, Under Secretary, National Protection and Programs Directorate, Department of Homeland Security, before the House Committee on Energy and Commerce, Subcommittee on Environment and the Economy, February 3, 2012.

Internal Review of CFATS Program

A series of challenges internal to the Infrastructure Security Compliance Division (ISCD), which implements CFATS regulations, led to an internal review of ISCD. These challenges included problems with the assignment of regulated chemical facilities to risk tiers and issues with respect to locality pay.[33] In December 2010, NPPD initiated a management review of ISCD through the NPPD Office of Compliance and Security. In July 2011, new leadership took charge of ISCD and, at the direction of Under Secretary Beers, began a review of the goals, challenges, and potential corrective actions to improve program performance.[34] In November 2011, ISCD leadership presented Under Secretary Beers with a report containing the results of both reviews. According to DHS, the report was intended as a candid, internal assessment that focused predominantly on the challenges faced by ISCD rather than on the program's successes and opportunities.[35]

At the time of the report, DHS had received approximately 4,200 site security plans but had not yet approved any. The review report identified several factors that contributed to this lack of success. These factors included the inability to perform compliance inspections and the lack of an established records management system to document key decisions were identified.[36] Other challenges facing ISCD reportedly include human resource issues, such as having employees with insufficient qualifications and work training, erroneous impressions of inspector roles and responsibilities, and the use of contractors to perform inherently governmental work.[37] Additional reported challenges include difficulty in quickly altering workplace requirements,[38] resolving personnel security requirements,[39] detailing site security compliance inspections,[40] managing workplace behavior and perceptions,[41] and dealing with a unionized workforce.[42] Additionally, ISCD lacked a system for tracking the usage of consumable supplies, potentially allowing for

---

[33] Oral testimony of Rand Beers, Under Secretary, National Protection and Programs Directorate, Department of Homeland Security, before the House Committee on Energy and Commerce, Subcommittee on Environment and the Economy, February 3, 2012.

[34] Personal communication with Department of Homeland Security, January 5, 2012.

[35] Oral testimony of David Wulf, Deputy Director, Infrastructure Security Compliance Division, National Protection and Programs Directorate, Department of Homeland Security, before the House Committee on Energy and Commerce, Subcommittee on Environment and the Economy, February 3, 2012.

[36] Government Accountability Office, *Critical Infrastructure Protection: DHS Is Taking Action to Better Manage Its Chemical Security Program, but It Is Too Early to Assess Results,* GAO-12-515T, July 26, 2012.

[37] Statements by Representative Gene Green during a hearing of the House Committee on Energy and Commerce, Subcommittee on Environment and the Economy, February 3, 2012, and Mike Levine, "EXCLUSIVE: Beset by Strife at Chemical Security Office, DHS Internal Report Claims Anti-Terrorism Program Now in Jeopardy," *FoxNews.com,* December 21, 2011.

[38] Mike Levine, "EXCLUSIVE: Beset by Strife at Chemical Security Office, DHS Internal Report Claims Anti-Terrorism Program Now in Jeopardy," *FoxNews.com,* December 21, 2011.

[39] Statements by Representative Gene Green during a hearing of the House Committee on Energy and Commerce, Subcommittee on Environment and the Economy, February 3, 2012.

[40] Statements by Representative Cassidy during a hearing of the House Committee on Energy and Commerce, Subcommittee on Environment and the Economy, February 3, 2012.

[41] Statements by Representative Gardner during a hearing of the House Committee on Energy and Commerce, Subcommittee on Environment and the Economy, February 3, 2012.

[42] Statements by Representative Gardner during a hearing of the House Committee on Energy and Commerce, Subcommittee on Environment and the Economy, February 3, 2012.

waste fraud and abuse;[43] faced challenges in hiring new qualified individuals; and suffered from a lack of morale.[44]

The memorandum identified three top priorities to address the challenges addressing ISCD:

- clearing the backlog of site security plans;

- developing a chemical inspection process; and

- addressing ISCD statutory responsibilities for regulating ammonium nitrate and managing personnel surety as part of the CFATS program.[45]

The ISCD has established a working group to look at potential legislative and regulatory changes and developed an action plan with discrete action items to address these challenges. In addition to the action plan, NPPD has requested ISCD leadership to provide milestones and a schedule for completion of the action plan tasks. The ISCD is implementing this plan with the oversight of NPPD leadership.[46] The DHS expects to assess the ongoing success of the action plan and revise it as necessary.[47] According to GAO, ISCD has developed at least eight sequential versions of the action plan, updating each additional version, and in some cases adding additional detail, milestones, or timelines.[48]

The DHS reports it has completed 59 of the 95 action items included in the action plan.[49] The ISCD has implemented an interim review process for site security plans with a goal of formalizing a new review process by July 2012.[50] To comply with items in the action plan, ISCD has updated its internal policy and guidance materials for inspections, created a monthly ISCD newsletter, promoted staff engagement and dialogue, provided additional supervisory training and guidance, and attempting to hire a permanent leadership team. In addition, NPPD is overseeing review of the process by which ISCD assigns risk tiers to regulated facilities.

---

[43] Statements by Representative Shimkus during a hearing of the House Committee on Energy and Commerce, Subcommittee on Environment and the Economy, February 3, 2012.

[44] Statements by Representative Gene Green during a hearing of the House Committee on Energy and Commerce, Subcommittee on Environment and the Economy, February 3, 2012.

[45] Government Accountability Office, *Critical Infrastructure Protection: DHS Is Taking Action to Better Manage Its Chemical Security Program, but It Is Too Early to Assess Results,* GAO-12-515T, July 26, 2012.

[46] ISCD program leadership meets with the Principal NPPD Deputy Under Secretary at least weekly to discuss progress on the action plan. Oral testimony of Rand Beers, Under Secretary, National Protection and Programs Directorate, Department of Homeland Security, before the House Committee on Energy and Commerce, Subcommittee on Environment and the Economy, February 3, 2012.

[47] Personal communication with Department of Homeland Security, January 5, 2012.

[48] Government Accountability Office, *Critical Infrastructure Protection: DHS Is Taking Action to Better Manage Its Chemical Security Program, but It Is Too Early to Assess Results,* GAO-12-515T, July 26, 2012.

[49] The GAO reports that DHS had completed 38 items as of June 2012. The DHS attributes this difference to ongoing work. Government Accountability Office, *Critical Infrastructure Protection: DHS Is Taking Action to Better Manage Its Chemical Security Program, but It Is Too Early to Assess Results,* GAO-12-567T, September 11, 2012. See also Testimony of Suzanne Spaulding, Deputy Under Secretary, National Protection and Programs Directorate, Department of Homeland Security, before the House Committee on Appropriations, Subcommittee on Homeland Security, July 26, 2012.

[50] Government Accountability Office, *Critical Infrastructure Protection: DHS Is Taking Action to Better Manage Its Chemical Security Program, but It Is Too Early to Assess Results,* GAO-12-515T, July 26, 2012.

The GAO has reviewed DHS progress on the action plan and stated that "ISCD appears to be heading in the right direction, but it is too early to tell if individual items are having their desired effect because ISCD is in the early stages of implementing corrective actions and has not established performance measures to assess results."[51] The GAO provides several caveats to its assessment, including that it did not have available documentary evidence about the causes of the issues identified in the ISCD memorandum. Notably, GAO states, "Program officials did not maintain records of key decisions and the basis for those decisions during the early years of the program."[52]

Policy Issues

Previous congressional discussion on chemical facility security raised several contentious policy issues.[53] Some issues, such as whether DHS has sufficient funds to adequately oversee chemical facility security; whether federal chemical facility security regulations should preempt state regulations; and how much chemical security information individuals may share outside of the facility and the federal government, will exist even if Congress extends the existing statutory authority without changes. Other issues, such as what facilities DHS should regulate as a chemical facility and whether DHS should require chemical facilities to adopt or consider adopting inherently safer technologies, may be more likely addressed if Congress chooses to revise or expand existing authority.

Adequacy of Funds and Efforts

The regulation establishes an oversight structure that relies on DHS personnel inspecting chemical facilities and ascertaining whether regulated entities have implemented their approved site security plans. Although the use of performance-based measures, where chemical facilities have flexibility in how to achieve the required security performance, may reduce some demands on the regulated entities, it may also require greater training and judgment on the part of DHS inspectors. Inspecting the regulated facilities likely will be costly. Congressional oversight has raised the question of whether DHS has requested and received appropriated funds sufficient to hire and retain the staff necessary to perform the required compliance inspections[54] and whether DHS has properly managed the appropriated funds received.

---

[51] Government Accountability Office, *Critical Infrastructure Protection: DHS Is Taking Action to Better Manage Its Chemical Security Program, but It Is Too Early to Assess Results,* GAO-12-515T, July 26, 2012.

[52] Government Accountability Office, *Critical Infrastructure Protection: DHS Is Taking Action to Better Manage Its Chemical Security Program, but It Is Too Early to Assess Results,* GAO-12-515T, July 26, 2012.

[53] Congressional policymakers have debated chemical facility security issues since at least the 106th Congress.

[54] See, for example, House Committee on Homeland Security, Subcommittee on Transportation Security and Infrastructure Protection, *Chemical Security: The Implementation of the Chemical Facility Anti-Terrorism Standards and the Road Ahead,* 110th Congress, December 12, 2007, and H.Rept. 112-492, accompanying H.R. 5855, Department of Homeland Security Appropriations Bill, 2013.

Sufficiency of Infrastructure and Workforce

The DHS may face challenges when creating the necessary infrastructure to perform nationwide inspections. As stated by DHS when describing its efforts to hire, train, and deploy an inspector cadre and support staff:

> Infrastructure Security Inspectors, located in up to 10 primary field offices across the Nation, will inspect and ensure regulatory compliance at facilities covered by the CFATS regulation, including site security plan approval and maintaining respective inspection and audit schedule. Creating a fully functional cadre will require not just recruiting and training staff, but also procurement of communications and [information technology] equipment (laptops, blackberries, etc.) to facilitate work efforts while conducting inspections and traveling, but also the acquisition of office space and equipment, government vehicles, support staff, safety equipment and clothing, and support for frequent travel.[55]

The degree to which funds meet agency needs likely depends on factors external and internal to DHS. External factors include the number of regulated facilities and the sufficiency of security plan implementation. Internal factors include the ratio between headquarters staff and field inspectors; the risk tiers of the regulated facilities; and the timetable for implementation of inspections. Once the DHS determines the tiers of all regulated facilities and their associated timetables, DHS may be able to more comprehensively determine its resource needs.[56] Now that DHS has begun implementation of these requirements, it may be able to provide further estimates of both funding and staff requirements. According to the committee report accompanying S. 3216, Department of Homeland Security Appropriations Bill, 2013, NPPD will complete during FY2012 a detailed manpower and systems review that will identify the total number of inspectors. A key factor may be the success in training inspectors to perform CFATS inspections, given the reported difficulties in developing effective inspector training combined with the requirements of a new regulatory program.

Rate of Inspection

As of September 2012, two chemical facilities have completed the CFATS process, which starts with information submission by chemical facilities and finishes with inspection and approval of security measures by DHS.[57] The DHS states that the first authorization inspection was conducted in 2010, and as of September 2012, DHS has conducted 19 authorization inspections.[58] According to the report accompanying H.R. 5855, Department of Homeland Security Appropriations Bill, 2013, DHS projects that it will require almost seven years of inspections to approve and inspect

---

[55] Department of Homeland Security, National Protection and Programs Directorate, Infrastructure Protection and Information Security, *Fiscal Year 2009 Congressional Justification*, p. IPIS-41.

[56] Congress required DHS in FY2006 and FY2007 to report on the resources needed to create and implement mandatory security requirements. See P.L. 109-295, Department of Homeland Security Appropriations Act, 2007, and H.Rept. 109-241, accompanying P.L. 109-90, Department of Homeland Security Appropriations Act, 2006.

[57] Testimony of Rand Beers, Under Secretary, National Protection and Programs Directorate, Department of Homeland Security, before the House Committee on Energy and Commerce, Subcommittee on Environment and the Economy, September 11, 2012.

[58] Oral Testimony of David Wulf, Director, Infrastructure Security Compliance Division, National Protection and Programs Directorate, Department of Homeland Security, before the House Committee on Energy and Commerce, Subcommittee on Environment and the Economy, September 11, 2012.

---

all regulated facilities.[59] Some policymakers have expressed surprise at the pace of inspection and questioned whether DHS should continue at the current pace or accelerate the compliance process.[60] Several factors likely complicate and slow the inspection process. One factor appears to be the internal operations of the DHS implementing office. Another factor appears to be that the information facilities submit in site security plans may not provide what DHS views as necessary detail to evaluate compliance.[61] Rather than reject these site security plans, DHS implemented an additional inspection function, a pre-authorization inspection, to allow DHS to gather the necessary information from regulated facilities.

While pre-authorization inspections may lead to higher quality site security plan submissions, they appear to be a significant drain on DHS resources. In principle, such pre-authorization inspections may lower the future authorization inspection burden, as CFATS inspectors will be familiar with security measures at the chemical facility. Such familiarity may hasten the actual authorization inspection.

The DHS has also suggested that pre-authorization inspections are most necessary at higher risk tier facilities, due to the complexity of the facility, the potential presence of multiple chemicals of interest, and the more stringent risk-based performance standards that apply. Lower risk tier facilities may not need pre-authorization inspections both because of their comparative simplicity and because inspectors may develop best practices through the pre-authorization inspections of higher tiered facilities.

Some policymakers have questioned whether the low inspection rate is due to constraints in the number of chemical facility security inspectors hired by DHS or the availability of appropriated funding. The CFATS regulation states that DHS will inspect the implementation of site security plans at all facilities and requires that facilities resubmit their site security plan every two years for Tier 1 and Tier 2 facilities or three years for Tier 3 and Tier 4 facilities.[62] This requires DHS to perform approximately 1,700 inspections annually to inspect each facility's implementation of its site security plan. The DHS has asserted that inspections require two or more inspectors and approximately one week to perform.[63]

The DHS appears to have requested sufficient inspectors to manage the workload associated with a reinspection cycle of every two years for top tier facilities and every three years for lower tier facilities, but such a staffing level may be insufficient to address the large number of initial regulatory submissions or a more frequent reinspection cycle.[64] This level of staffing would

---

[59] H.Rept. 112-493, accompanying H.R. 5855, Department of Homeland Security Appropriations Bill, 2013, p. 101.

[60] Monica Hatcher, "Why Chemical Plants Are Vulnerable to Terrorism," *Houston Chronicle*, April 5, 2010.

[61] For example, see Department of Homeland Security, *Chemical Facility Anti-Terrorism Standards Site Security Plans and Preliminary Inspections, NASTTPO Annual Meeting*, May 12, 2010; and W. Koch, Air Products, *Overview of DHS CFATS Pre Authorization Visit*, July 7, 2010.

[62] Other DHS documents have provided different inspection timeframes. In 2011, DHS stated its expectation that, when at full operational capability, it would inspect Tier 1 facilities annually, Tier 2 facilities every two years, and a prioritized selection of 10% of Tier 3 and Tier 4 facilities each year (Department of Homeland Security, *Annual Performance Report Fiscal Years 2010 – 2012; Appendix A: Measure Descriptions and Data Collection Methodologies*, p. 8). In 2011, DHS stated that it plans to inspect compliance at Tier 1 facilities annually (Department of Homeland Security, National Protection and Programs Directorate, Infrastructure Protection and Information Security, *Fiscal Year 2012 Congressional Justification*, p. 26).

[63] Department of Homeland Security, *The Chemical Facility Anti-Terrorism Standards—Update for the Chemical Sector Security Summit*, June 29, 2009.

[64] CRS calculation assuming two inspectors per inspection and one inspection per week.

---

appear to require approximately a full cycle of inspections to reduce the backlog created from the initial site security plan submissions. If DHS were to hire additional inspectors, it might reduce the backlog of site security plans but also run the risk of having additional unnecessary staff in future years. The DHS might hire temporary or short-term staff to augment the inspector cadre, but the need to train such employees for CFATS-specific inspections may pose challenges.

Finally, because DHS has focused on inspecting those facilities in the highest risk tier, it potentially faces the most complicated inspection environments. Inspections of lower risk tier facilities may pose fewer complications, take less time, and involve fewer inspectors. If so, DHS might quickly and substantially increase the number of facilities inspected by focusing efforts on lower tier facilities. Through this approach, DHS might gain insight and experience among the inspector cadre while reducing some national risk.[65]

Federal Preemption of State Activities

The original statute did not expressly address the issue of federal preemption of state and local chemical facility security statute or regulation. When DHS issued regulations establishing the CFATS program, DHS asserted that the CFATS regulations would preempt state and local chemical facility security statute or regulation that conflicted with, hindered, posed an obstacle, or frustrated the purposes of the federal regulation.[66] Subsequent to the release of the regulation, Congress amended DHS's statutory authority to state that only in the case of an "actual conflict" would the federal regulation preempt state authority.[67] Few states have established independent chemical facility security regulatory programs, and conflict between the federal and state activities has not yet occurred.[68] The DHS did not identify any state programs that conflict with the CFATS regulations.[69] The DHS has also not altered its regulatory language in response to the statutory amendment.

Advocates for federal preemption call for a uniform security framework across the nation. They assert that a "patchwork" of regulations might develop if states independently develop additional chemical facility security regulations.[70] Variation in security requirements might lead to differing regulatory compliance costs, and companies might suffer competitive disadvantage based on their geographic location.

Supporters of a state's right to regulate chemical facility security claim that the federal regulation should be a minimum standard with which all regulated entities must comply. They assert that DHS should allow states to develop more stringent regulations than the federal regulations. They claim such regulations would increase security. Some supporters of state regulation suggest that more stringent, conflicting state regulations should preempt the federal regulations.[71] Such a case

---

[65] It should be noted that all facilities regulated under CFATS are by definition high-risk chemical facilities and that a lower or higher risk tier is relative to other high-risk chemical facilities.

[66] 72 *Federal Register* 17688–17745 (April 9, 2007) at 17739.

[67] Section 534, P.L. 110-161, Consolidated Appropriations Act, 2008.

[68] Several states, including New Jersey, Maryland, and New York, have implemented laws addressing security at chemical facilities.

[69] 72 *Federal Register* 17688–17745 (April 9, 2007) at 17727.

[70] See, for example, National Association of Chemical Distributors, "NACD Key Issue: Chemical Facility Security," *Key Issues 2009 Washington Fly-In 111th Congress*.

[71] For example, in the 111th Congress, Representative Rothman asked Secretary of Homeland Security Napolitano, (continued...)

might occur if a state regulation mandated the use of a particular security approach at chemical facilities, conflicting with the federal regulation that adopts a performance-based, rather than prescriptive, approach. The desire to retain industries that might relocate if faced with increased regulation arguably would temper state inclinations to require overly stringent or incompatible regulations.

Some policymakers may assert that chemical facility security should be left to the states rather than be implemented by the federal government. If Congress allows the statutory authority to expire and does not appropriate funds for the further implementation of CFATS, the federal authority would lapse and states would again be responsible for regulating chemical facility security.

Transparency of Process

The CFATS process involves determining chemical facility vulnerabilities and developing security plans to address them. Information developed in this process is not widely or openly disseminated. The CFATS program categorizes this information as CVI and provides penalties for its disclosure. Some advocates have argued for greater transparency in the CFATS process, even if the program does not provide detailed information regarding potential vulnerabilities and specific security measures. They assert that those individuals living in surrounding communities require such information to plan effectively and make choices in an emergency.[72]

The current statute and regulation prohibit public disclosure of security-related information. Only specific "covered persons" may access CVI. While acknowledging a legitimate homeland security need to limit dissemination of security information, some policymakers have questioned whether such limitations hinder other efforts. For example, first responders and community representatives have highlighted how such information protection regimes may impede emergency response and the ability of those in the surrounding community to react to emergency situations at the chemical facility.[73] Additionally, worker representatives have raised concerns that these limitations and the lack of mandated inclusion of worker representatives may impede worker input into security plans.[74]

(...continued)

> And in particular, there was language enacted in 2008 which said that the states could have their own regulations with regard to securing chemical plant facilities unless there was a conflict with the federal requirements. Might it be time to revisit that language to allow each state to have its own chemical plant security regulations, even stricter than a national minimum standard, even if they conflict?

("House Appropriations Subcommittee on Homeland Security Holds Hearing on the Department of Homeland Security," *CQ Congressional Transcripts*, May 12, 2009.)

[72] OMB Watch and Public Citizen, "Chemical Facility Anti-Terrorism Standards, Department of Homeland Security, DHS-2006-0073," *Letter*, February 7, 2007.

[73] Testimony of Joseph Crawford, Chief of Police, City Saint Albans, West Virginia, before the House Committee on Energy and Commerce, Subcommittee on Oversight and Investigations, April 21, 2009; and testimony of Kent Carper, President, Kanawha County Commission, Kanawha County, West Virginia, before the House Committee on Energy and Commerce, Subcommittee on Oversight and Investigations, April 21, 2009.

[74] See, for example, testimony of Glenn Erwin, United Steelworkers International Union, before the Senate Committee on Homeland Security and Governmental Affairs, July 13, 2005.

The current information protection regimes for chemical facility security information, CVI under CFATS and Sensitive Security Information (SSI) under the Maritime Transportation Security Act (MTSA), do not contain penalties for incorrectly marking information as protected. Only disclosure of correctly marked information is penalized. Additionally, the chemical facility is responsible for identifying and appropriately marking protected information. These information markings only would be assessed in the case of dispute. As was asserted during congressional oversight, this disparity may lead to a tendency by regulated entities, in order to protect themselves against potential liability or scrutiny, to erroneously limit dissemination of information that should be made available to the public.[75]

Congressional investigation indicated that documents related to the 2007 explosion at a Bayer CropScience chemical facility in West Virginia were incorrectly labeled as protected from disclosure.[76] The DHS regulated this chemical facility under MTSA, not CFATS.[77] In this case, security information was protected from disclosure as SSI, an information protection regime similar to CVI. Company officials broadly applied SSI markings to facility documents partly in hopes of avoiding a public debate on the use and storage of particular chemicals at the facility.[78] This revelation led to questions regarding the application and oversight of such protective markings.

Additionally, the existing statute contains no provisions explicitly protecting or allowing for concerned covered persons to divulge CVI or to challenge the categorization of information as protected in an attempt to inform authorities about security vulnerabilities or other weaknesses. Depending on the circumstances, those individuals might be penalized for their disclosure of protected information. The CFATS regulations, reflecting this inherent tension, provide for a point of contact to which such information might be revealed, but also state "Section 550 did not give DHS authority to provide whistleblower protection, and so DHS has not incorporated specific whistleblower protections into this regulation."[79]

Definition of Chemical Facility

The DHS regulates both entities that possess and entities that manufacture chemicals of interest. Thus, the term chemical facility encompasses many types of facilities, including agricultural facilities, universities, and others. With DHS defining chemical facilities according to possession of a chemical of interest, facilities not part of the chemical manufacturing and distributing chain have become regulated facilities. Stakeholders have expressed concern that the number of entities so regulated might be unwieldy and that the regulatory program might focus on many chemical facilities that pose little risk rather than on those facilities that pose more substantial risk. For

---

[75] "House Energy and Commerce Subcommittee on Oversight and Investigations Holds Hearing on the Bayer CropScience Facility Explosion," *CQ Congressional Transcripts*, April 21, 2009.

[76] For example, see "House Energy and Commerce Subcommittee on Oversight and Investigations Holds Hearing on the Bayer CropScience Facility Explosion," *CQ Congressional Transcripts*, April 21, 2009.

[77] The DHS regulates for security purposes chemical facilities located in ports under the Maritime Transportation Security Act of 2002 (P.L. 107-295). The chemical facility security statute exempts chemical facilities regulated under MTSA.

[78] Testimony of William B. Buckner, President and Chief Executive Officer of Bayer CropScience, before the House Committee on Energy and Commerce, Subcommittee on Oversight and Investigations, April 21, 2009.

[79] 72 *Federal Register* 17688–17745 (April 9, 2007) at 17718.

example, during the rulemaking process, DHS received commentary and revised its regulatory threshold for possession of propane, stating:

> DHS, however, set the [screening threshold quantities] for propane in this final rule at 60,000 pounds. Sixty thousand pounds is the estimated maximum amount of propane that non-industrial propane customers, such as restaurants and farmers, typically use. The Department believes that non-industrial users, especially those in rural areas, do not have the potential to create a significant risk to human life or health as would industrial users. The Department has elected, at this time, to focus efforts on large commercial propane establishments but may, after providing the public with an opportunity for notice and comment, extend its [CFATS] screening efforts to smaller facilities in the future. This higher [screening threshold quantity] will focus DHS's security screening effort on industrial and major consumers, regional suppliers, bulk retail, and storage sites and away from non-industrial propane customers.[80]

Similarly, academic institutions have asserted that DHS should not apply CFATS regulations to them because of the dispersed nature of chemical holdings at colleges and universities. These institutions claim that regulatory compliance costs would not be commensurate with the risk reduction.[81] While the regulatory compliance costs likely decrease at lower risk tiers compared to higher risk tiers, all regulated entities bear compliance costs as continued annual expenses.

As mentioned above, the statutory authority underlying CFATS exempts several types of facilities, including water and wastewater treatment facilities. The federal government does not regulate water and wastewater treatment facilities for chemical security purposes. Instead, current chemical security efforts at water and wastewater treatment facilities are voluntary in nature.[82] Some advocacy groups have called for inclusion of currently exempt facilities, such as water and wastewater treatment facilities.[83] Some drinking water and wastewater treatment facilities possess large amounts of potentially hazardous chemicals, such as chlorine, for purposes such as disinfection.[84] Advocates for their inclusion in security regulations cite the presence of such potentially hazardous chemicals and their relative proximity to population centers as reasons to mandate security measures for such facilities. In contrast, representatives of the water sector point to the critical role that water and wastewater treatment facilities have in daily life. They caution against including these facilities in the existing regulatory framework because of the potential for undue public impacts. They cite, for example, loss of basic fire protection and sanitation services if the federal government orders a water or wastewater utility to cease operations for security reasons or failure to comply with regulation.[85]

---

[80] 72 *Federal Register* 65396–65435 (November 20, 2007) at 65406.

[81] 72 *Federal Register* 65396–65435 (November 20, 2007) at 65412.

[82] Congress required certain drinking water facilities to perform vulnerability assessments and develop emergency response plans through section 401 of P.L. 107-188, the Public Health Security and Bioterrorism Preparedness and Response Act of 2002. For more information on drinking water security activities, see CRS Report RL31294, *Safeguarding the Nation's Drinking Water: EPA and Congressional Actions*, by Mary Tiemann.

[83] See, for example, Paul Orum and Reece Rushing, Center for American Progress, *Chemical Security 101: What You Don't Have Can't Leak, or Be Blown Up by Terrorists*, November 2008; and testimony of Philip J. Crowley, Senior Fellow and Director of Homeland Security, Center for American Progress, before the House Committee on Energy and Commerce, Subcommittee on Environment and Hazardous Materials, June 12, 2008.

[84] See U.S. Environmental Protection Agency, *Factoids: Drinking Water and Ground Water Statistics for 2008*, EPA 816-K-08-004, November 2008; and U.S. Environmental Protection Agency, *Clean Watersheds Needs Survey 2004: Report to Congress*, January 2008.

[85] American Water Works Association, "Chemical Facility Security," *Fact Sheet*, 2009, online at (continued...)

If Congress were to remove the drinking water and wastewater treatment facility exemption, the number of regulated facilities might substantially increase, placing additional burdens on the CFATS program. The United States contains approximately 52,000 community water systems and 16,500 wastewater treatment facilities.[86] These facilities vary substantially in size and service. The number of regulated facilities would depend on the criteria used to determine inclusion, such as chemical possession or number of individuals served. It is likely that only a subset of these facilities would meet a regulatory threshold.[87] In 2011, a DHS official testified that approximately 6,000 such facilities would likely meet the CFATS threshold.[88]

Use of Inherently Safer Technologies

Previous debate on chemical facility security has included whether to mandate the adoption or consideration of changes in chemical processes to reduce the potential consequences following a successful attack on a chemical facility. Suggestions for such changes have included reducing the amount of chemical stored onsite and changing the chemicals used. In previous congressional debate, these approaches have been referred to as inherently safer technologies or methods to reduce the consequences of a terrorist attack.

A fundamental challenge for inherently safer technologies is how to compare one technology with its potential replacement. It is challenging to unequivocally state that one technology is inherently safer than the other without adequate metrics. Risk factors may exist outside of the comparison framework.[89] Some experts have asserted that the metrics for comparing industrial processes are not yet fully established and need additional research and study.[90] The National Academies have recommended that DHS support research and development to foster cost-effective, inherently

---

(...continued)

http://www.awwa.org/files/GovtPublicAffairs/PDF/2009Security.pdf. For more information on security issues in the water infrastructure sector, see CRS Report RL32189, *Terrorism and Security Issues Facing the Water Infrastructure Sector*, by Claudia Copeland.

[86] See U.S. Environmental Protection Agency, *Factoids: Drinking Water and Ground Water Statistics for 2008*, EPA 816-K-08-004, November 2008; and U.S. Environmental Protection Agency, *Clean Watersheds Needs Survey 2004: Report to Congress*, January 2008. For comparison, more than 38,000 chemical facilities filed a Top-Screen under CFATS.

[87] For example, the number of individuals served by the drinking water facility might be used as a regulatory criterion. Section 401 of the Public Health Security and Bioterrorism Preparedness and Response Act of 2002 (P.L. 107-188) mandated drinking water facilities serving more than 3,300 individuals develop an emergency response plan and perform a vulnerability assessment. Approximately 8,400 community water systems met this requirement at that time. For more information on drinking water security activities, see CRS Report RL31294, *Safeguarding the Nation's Drinking Water: EPA and Congressional Actions*, by Mary Tiemann.

[88] Oral testimony of Rand Beers, Under Secretary, National Protection and Programs Directorate, Department of Homeland Security, before the House Committee on Homeland Security, Subcommittee on Cybersecurity, Infrastructure Protection, and Security Technologies, February 11, 2011.

[89] For example, the replacement of hydrogen fluoride with sulfuric acid for refinery processing would replace a more toxic chemical with a less toxic one. In this case, experts estimate that equivalent processing capacity would require twenty-five times more sulfuric acid. Thus, more chemical storage facilities and transportation would be required, potentially posing different dangers than atmospheric release to the surrounding community. Determining which chemical process had less overall risk might require considering factors both internal and external to the chemical facility and the surrounding community. See testimony of M. Sam Mannan, Director, Mary Kay O'Connor Process Safety Center, Texas A&M University, before the House Committee on Homeland Security, December 12, 2007.

[90] Testimony of M. Sam Mannan, Director, Mary Kay O'Connor Process Safety Center, Texas A&M University, before the House Committee on Homeland Security, December 12, 2007.

---

safer chemistries and chemical processes.[91] The National Academies has identified as a potential concern that inherently safer process analyses may become narrowly focused and its outcomes inappropriately weighted.[92] A facility might consider many additional factors beyond homeland security implications when weighing the applicability and benefit of switching from one process to another. These factors include cost, technical challenges regarding implementation in specific situations, supply chain impacts, quality and availability of end products, and indirect effects on workers.[93]

Supporters of adopting these approaches as a way to improve chemical facility security argue that reducing or removing these chemicals from a facility will reduce the incentive to attack the facility. They suggest that reducing the consequences of a release also lowers the threat from terrorist attack and mitigates the risk to the surrounding populace. They point to facilities that have voluntarily changed amounts of chemicals on hand or chemical processes in use as examples that facilities can implement such an approach in a cost-effective, practical fashion.[94]

Opponents of mandating what proponents call inherently safer technologies question the validity of the approach as a security tool and the government's ability to effectively oversee its implementation. Industrial entities assert that process safety engineers within the regulated industry already employ such approaches and that these are safety, not security, methods. They assert that process safety experts and business executives should determine the applicability and financial practicality of changing existing processes at specific chemical facilities.[95] A 2011 industry survey stated that, of those respondents that assessed using alternative chemicals or processes, 66.4% determined such alternatives were not technically feasible.[96] Opponents of an inherently safer technology mandate also state concern that few existing alternative approaches are well understood with regard to their unanticipated side effects. They claim that researchers should continue to study these alternative approaches rather than immediately apply them, since unanticipated side effects could injure business and other interests.[97] A third opposing view questions whether the federal government contains the required technical expertise to adjudicate

---

[91] Committee on Assessing Vulnerabilities Related to the Nation's Chemical Infrastructure, National Research Council, *Terrorism and the Chemical Infrastructure: Protecting People and Reducing Vulnerabilities*, 2006.

[92] Committee on Inherently Safer Chemical Processes, National Research Council, *The Use of Methyl Isocyanate (MIC) at Bayer CropScience*, 2012.

[93] For further discussion on this issue, see Center for Chemical Process Safety, American Institute of Chemical Engineers, *Final Report: Definition for Inherently Safer Technology in Production, Transportation, Storage, and Use*, July 2010.

[94] See, for example, Paul Orum and Reece Rushing, Center for American Progress, *Preventing Toxic Terrorism: How Some Chemical Facilities Are Removing Danger to American Communities*, April 2006; and Paul Orum and Reece Rushing, Center for American Progress, *Chemical Security 101: What You Don't Have Can't Leak, or Be Blown Up by Terrorists*, November 2008.

[95] See, for example, testimony of Timothy J. Scott, Dow Chemical Company, before the House Committee on Homeland Security, Subcommittee on Cybersecurity, Infrastructure Protection, and Security Technologies, February 11, 2011; and testimony of Marty Durbin, Managing Director, Federal Affairs, American Chemistry Council, before the House Committee on Energy and Commerce, Subcommittee on Environment and Hazardous Materials, June 12, 2008.

[96] AcuTech Consulting Group, *A Survey of CFATS Progress in Securing the Chemical Sector*, September 6, 2011, p. 41.

[97] For example, EPA experts have pointed to the change by drinking water treatment facilities between two approved disinfectants—chlorine and chloramine—as correlated with an unexpected increase in levels of lead in drinking water due to increased corrosion. Government Accountability Office, *Lead in D.C. Drinking Water*, GAO-05-344, March 2005.

---

the practicality and benefit of alternative technological approaches. Holders of this view raise concerns that the federal government may not possess the required knowledge or expertise to judge whether a particular site can implement alternative technology, even if the alternative theoretically provides benefits over existing technology.[98]

The DHS has engaged in research and development activities within its Science and Technology (S&T) Directorate to develop a better understanding of inherently safer technology, including efforts to define inherently safer technology.[99] The NPPD has not adopted the results from these research and development efforts within its regulatory context. Congress has directed DHS to detail and report to Congress the Department's definition of inherently safer technology as it relates to chemical facilities under the purview of CFATS.[100]

Some industry representatives have asserted that an inherently safer technology mandate might have a potentially significant negative financial impact.[101] Regulated entities incur a cost when meeting existing CFATS requirements, and small businesses may be challenged to make necessary capital investments. In its interim final rule, DHS estimated that even without an inherently safer technology requirement CFATS "may have a significant economic impact on a substantial number of small entities."[102] Because of the performance-based nature of the regulatory requirement, it is difficult to detail the exact impact on small businesses.[103] Adding an inherently safer technology requirement might increase the cost of CFATS compliance and might disproportionately affect small entities not already incorporating such activities in their business processes. Policymakers in previous Congresses highlighted the issue of small business impact, especially in the context of requiring additional measures that might hurt productivity.

Policy Options

The statutory authority for CFATS expires on March 27, 2013. The Obama Administration has requested a one-year extension of this authority until October 4, 2013.[104] The 112th Congress may address chemical facility security through several options. Congress may increase its oversight of

---

[98] See, for example, testimony of M. Sam Mannan, Director, Mary Kay O'Connor Process Safety Center, Texas A&M University, before the House Committee on Homeland Security, Subcommittee on Cybersecurity, Infrastructure Protection, and Security Technologies, February 11, 2011; testimony of Dennis C. Hendershot, Staff Consultant, Center for Chemical Process Safety, American Institute of Chemical Engineers, before the Senate Committee on Environment and Public Works, June 21, 2006, S.Hrg. 109-1044; and testimony of Matthew Barmasse, Synthetic Organic Chemical Manufacturers Association, before the Senate Committee on Homeland Security and Governmental Affairs, July 13, 2005.

[99] The Chemical Security Analysis Center of the DHS S&T Directorate contracted with the Center for Chemical Process Safety of the American Institute of Chemical Engineers to develop a technically based definition for inherently safer technology. See Center for Chemical Process Safety, American Institute of Chemical Engineers, *Final Report: Definition for Inherently Safer Technology in Production, Transportation, Storage, and Use*, July 2010.

[100] H.Rept. 112-331, p. 986.

[101] Testimony of Stephen Poorman, International EHS Manager, FUJIFILM Imaging Colorants Ltd., on behalf of the Society of Chemical Manufacturers and Affiliates before the Senate Committee on Homeland Security and Governmental Affairs, March 3, 2010.

[102] 72 *Federal Register* 17688–17745 (April 9, 2007) at 17772.

[103] Department of Homeland Security, *Chemical Facility Anti-Terrorism Standards Interim Final Rule Regulatory Assessment*, DHS-2006-0073, April 1, 2007.

[104] Office of Management and Budget, The White House, *Budget of the United States Government, Fiscal Year 2013, Appendix*, p. 597.

DHS's efforts to implement this program. Congress might also take legislative action to extend further the existing statutory authority by revising or repealing its sunset provision; codify the existing regulations; amend the existing statutory authority; address existing programmatic activities; or restrict or expand the scope of chemical facility security regulation.

If Congress does not act and allows the statutory authority to expire, regulated entities may question the application and enforcement of the CFATS regulations. In the case where Congress allows the statutory authority to expire, but Congress appropriates funds for enforcing the CFATS program, DHS will likely be able to enforce the CFATS regulations. The Government Accountability Office (GAO) has found that in the case where a program's statutory authority expires, but Congress explicitly appropriates funding for it, the program may continue to operate without interruption.[105] If Congress allows the statutory authority to expire and also does not appropriate funding for implementing the CFATS program, the CFATS regulations will likely also lapse. In this case, the states would likely become the primary source of any chemical facility security regulation.

Increase Congressional Oversight

Interested Members of Congress or congressional committees might increase their oversight of the CFATS program. Historically, much of the congressional debate has considered legislative options to reauthorize the existing statute or authorize the CFATS program through a different statutory vehicle. Congressional committees have accepted the assurances of DHS officials regarding CFATS activities even as DHS failed to meet its self-established deadlines. With the program's critical self-assessment, congressional oversight may increase due to concerns about program performance, use of appropriations, and internal oversight.

The 112th Congress has held oversight hearings on DHS's implementation of the CFATS program. Following the results of the ISCD review memorandum, congressional oversight has additionally focused on DHS's progress in addressing identified management challenges. The GAO is currently reviewing the CFATS program management and plans on beginning a new engagement addressing mission-related issues.[106]

Maintain the Existing Regulatory Framework

The existing statutory authority places much of the CFATS regulatory framework at the discretion of the Secretary of Homeland Security. The DHS is still in the process of implementing these regulations and has not yet determined their effectiveness. Congressional oversight of their implementation, enforcement, and efficacy may play a key role in determining the sufficiency of the existing authority and regulations. Congress might choose to maintain the existing regulations by extending the statutory authority's sunset date or codifying the existing regulations. Also, as noted above, allowing the statutory authority to expire could in effect maintain the existing regulatory framework if Congress continues to fund implementation, although this might lead to litigation.

---

[105] Office of the General Counsel, General Accounting Office, *Principles of Federal Appropriations Law, Third Edition*, GAO-04-261SP, January, 2004, pp. 2-70–2-71.

[106] Government Accountability Office, *Critical Infrastructure Protection: DHS Is Taking Action to Better Manage Its Chemical Security Program, but It Is Too Early to Assess Results*, GAO-12-515T, July 26, 2012.

Extend the Sunset Date

Congressional policymakers might choose to extend the current statutory authority for a fixed or indefinite time. Congress has enacted a series of limited extensions of the statutory authority since its inception. The Obama Administration requested for FY2012 an extension of the statutory authority to October 4, 2013.[107] The Consolidated Appropriations Act, 2012 (P.L. 112-74) extends the statutory authority through October 4, 2012. Extending the existing statutory authority may provide regulated entities continuity and protect them from losing benefits from those resources already expended in regulatory compliance. An extension may allow assessment of the efficacy of the existing regulations and inclusion of this information in any future attempts to revise or extend DHS's statutory authority. Moreover, since DHS is in the process of implementing current regulations, some policymakers argue for a simple extension without changing statutory requirements.

In addition to requesting an extension of the statutory authority, the Obama Administration also supports enacting a permanent statutory authority.[108] Congress might make the existing program permanent by removing the sunset date entirely. Some chemical manufacturers support converting the existing program into a permanent program.[109] The removal of the sunset date would maintain the current discretion granted to the Secretary of Homeland Security to develop regulations and might allow assessment of the efficacy of the existing regulations. Making the existing statute permanent would provide consistency in authority and remove the statutory pressure to reauthorize the program. In contrast, the presence of a sunset date for the statutory authority increases the likelihood of congressional attention to chemical facility security as a legislative topic. Some advocates who wish for more regular congressional review of the statute might oppose removing the sunset date.

Codify the Existing Regulations

Congressional policymakers might choose to affirm the existing regulations by codifying them or their principles in statute. Such codification could reduce the discretion of the Secretary of Homeland Security to alter the CFATS regulations in the future. The existing statutory authority grants broad discretion to the Secretary to develop many elements of the CFATS regulations. Future Secretaries may choose to alter its structure or approach and still comply with the existing statute. Policymakers might identify specific components of the existing regulation that they wish any future regulation to retain and codify those portions. Specifying these components might limit the ability of the Secretary to react to changing circumstance, gained experience, and new knowledge. On the other hand, the codified portions might enhance the regulated community's ability to plan for future expenses and requirements.

---

[107] Office of Management and Budget, The White House, *Budget of the United States Government, Fiscal Year 2012, Appendix*, p. 553.

[108] Oral testimony of Rand Beers, Under Secretary, National Protection and Programs Directorate, Department of Homeland Security, before the House Committee on Homeland Security, Subcommittee on Cybersecurity, Infrastructure Protection, and Security Technologies, February 11, 2011.

[109] Randy Dearth and Cal Dooley, "Commentary: Taking Chemical Plant Security in Pittsburgh Seriously," *Pittsburgh Post-Gazette*, May 27, 2009.

Alter the Existing Statutory Authority

Congressional policymakers might choose to alter the existing statutory authority to modify the existing regulations, address stakeholder concerns, or broadly change the regulatory program.

Accelerate or Decelerate Compliance Activities

The DHS bases its schedule for facility CFATS compliance on the chemical facility's assigned risk tier. Those chemical facilities assigned to higher risk tiers have a more accelerated compliance and resubmission schedule than those assigned to lower risk tiers. Congressional policymakers might attempt to accelerate the compliance schedule by increasing funding available to DHS for CFATS, thereby increasing the ability of DHS to provide feedback to regulated entities, review submissions, and inspect facilities filing site security plans. Additional funding might reduce or mitigate inefficiencies or delays related to DHS processing of submissions.

Alternatively, policymakers might provide DHS with the authority to use third parties as CFATS inspectors. The DHS could then augment the number of CFATS inspectors to meet increased demand or delegate inspection authority to state and local governments. Third-party inspectors might allow DHS to draw on expertise outside of the federal government in assessing the efficacy of the implemented site security activities. The DHS may need to define the roles and responsibilities of these inspectors and how DHS will assess and accredit their qualifications. The DHS has stated its intent to issue a rulemaking regarding the use of third-party inspectors but has not yet done so.[110] The use of third-party inspectors might lead to concerns about equal treatment of chemical facilities by different third-party inspectors, and questions about whether homeland security inspections of this type are an inherently governmental responsibility that only federal employees should perform.

Finally, Congress might determine that DHS has sufficient resources to accelerate compliance activities but is restrained by some other procedural factor. Congressional policymakers might direct DHS to streamline its review process, reduce the timeframe for response and interaction with regulated entities, or otherwise enact process improvements.

Congressional policymakers might choose to slow the implementation schedule of the chemical facility security regulations. Concern about the impact of the regulation on small businesses or other entities might lead to a decelerated compliance schedule. The DHS has already implemented select regulatory extensions for certain agricultural operations.[111] Congressional policymakers might direct DHS to provide longer submission, implementation, and resubmission timelines for those regulated entities that might suffer disproportionate economic burdens from compliance.

---

[110] 72 *Federal Register* 17688–17745 (April 9, 2007) at 17712.

[111] 73 *Federal Register* 1640 (January 9, 2008).

Incorporate Additional Facility Types

Policymakers might remove some or all of the statutory exclusions from the CFATS program. The DHS and the Environmental Protection Agency (EPA) have called for additional authorities to regulate water and wastewater treatment facilities:

> The Department of Homeland Security and the Environmental Protection Agency believe that there is an important gap in the framework for regulating the security of chemicals at water and wastewater treatment facilities in the United States. The authority for regulating the chemical industry purposefully excludes from its coverage water and wastewater treatment facilities. We need to work with the Congress to close this gap in the chemical security authorities in order to secure chemicals of interest at these facilities and protect the communities they serve. Water and wastewater treatment facilities that are determined to be high-risk due to the presence of chemicals of interest should be regulated for security in a manner that is consistent with the CFATS risk and performance-based framework while also recognizing the unique public health and environmental requirements and responsibilities of such facilities.[112]

The EPA has testified that the Obama Administration believes that EPA should be the lead agency for chemical security for both drinking water and wastewater systems, with DHS supporting EPA's efforts.[113] The EPA also supports providing states with an important role in regulating chemical security at water systems, including determinations, auditing, and inspecting.[114]

In addition, DHS supports modifying the existing exemption for (1) MTSA facilities to increase security at these facilities to the CFATS standard and (2) facilities regulated by the Nuclear Regulatory Commission to clarify the scope of the exemption.[115]

If Congress provides the executive branch with statutory authority to regulate water and wastewater treatment facilities for chemical security purposes, it may weigh several policy decisions. Among these choices are which facilities should be regulated; how stringent such security measures should be; what federal agency should oversee them; and whether compliance with these security measures is practicable given the public nature of many water and wastewater treatment facilities.

One option for congressional policymakers might be to include water and wastewater treatment facilities under the existing CFATS regulations, effectively removing the exemption currently in statute. This would place water and wastewater treatment facilities on par with other possessors

---

[112] Testimony of Benjamin H. Grumbles, Assistant Administrator for Water, U.S. Environmental Protection Agency before the House Committee on Energy and Commerce, Subcommittee on Environment and Hazardous Materials, June 12, 2008. See also testimony of Rand Beers, Under Secretary, National Protection and Programs Directorate, Department of Homeland Security, before the Senate Committee on Homeland Security and Governmental Affairs, March 3, 2010.

[113] Testimony of Peter S. Silva, Assistant Administrator for Water, Environmental Protection Agency, before the Senate Committee on Homeland Security and Governmental Affairs, March 3, 2010.

[114] Testimony of Peter S. Silva, Assistant Administrator for Water, Environmental Protection Agency, before the Senate Committee on Homeland Security and Governmental Affairs, March 3, 2010.

[115] Testimony of Rand Beers, Under Secretary, National Protection and Programs Directorate, Department of Homeland Security, before the Senate Committee on Homeland Security and Governmental Affairs, March 3, 2010. The DHS and the Nuclear Regulatory Commission have developed a memorandum of agreement regarding security at chemical facilities regulated by the Nuclear Regulatory Commission (*Memorandum of Understanding between the U.S. Department of Homeland Security and the U.S. Nuclear Regulatory Commission*, March 31, 2011).

of chemicals of interest. The DHS would provide oversight of all regulated chemical facilities.[116] Opponents might claim that activities under CFATS, such as vulnerability assessment, duplicate existing requirements under the Safe Drinking Water Act.[117] Also, opponents of such an approach cite the essential role that water and wastewater treatment facilities play in daily life and assert that several authorities available to DHS under CFATS, such as the ability to require a facility to cease operations, are inappropriate if applied to a municipal utility.[118]

Another option might be to grant statutory authority to regulate water and wastewater treatment facilities for security purposes to EPA or require DHS to consult with EPA regarding its regulation of water and wastewater treatment facilities. Since water treatment facilities must provide a vulnerability assessment to EPA, some facilities might view regulation under CFATS as redundant in this context. Some industry representatives have expressed concern regarding the effects of multiple agencies regulating security at drinking water and wastewater treatment facilities.[119] They assert that municipalities that operate both types of facilities might face conflicting regulations and guidance if different agencies regulate drinking water and wastewater treatment facilities. These stakeholders suggest that EPA retaining the lead for water and wastewater facilities would be more efficient. Following prior debate on chemical facility security, Congress provided statutory authority for chemical security to DHS. This separated DHS security responsibilities from the public health and safety responsibilities given to EPA. Providing one agency the authority to oversee safety and security operations may reduce the potential for redundancy and other inefficiencies but also might increase stakeholder reluctance to voluntarily consult on security issues.[120]

If policymakers assign responsibility for chemical facility security at different facilities to different agencies, each agency will promulgate separate rules. These rules may be similar or different depending on the agencies' statutory authority, interpretation of that authority, and ability of the regulated entities to comply as well as any interagency coordination that might occur. Congress may wish to assess the areas where such facilities are similar and different in order to provide authorities that meet any unique characteristics.

Any new regulation of drinking water and wastewater treatment facilities is likely to cause the regulated entities, and potentially the federal government, to incur some costs. Representatives of the water and wastewater sectors argue that local ratepayers will eventually bear the capital and ongoing costs incurred due to increased security measures.[121] Congressional policymakers may

---

[116] Those chemical facilities exempt from CFATS because they are regulated under MTSA are overseen by the Coast Guard, which is part of DHS. The DHS testified that 365 facilities are fully exempt from CFATS regulation due to compliance with MTSA, while 135 are partially exempt ("House Committee on Homeland Security Holds Hearing on the Chemical Facility Antiterrorism Act of 2009," *CQ Congressional Transcripts*, June 16, 2009).

[117] Section 1433 of the Safe Drinking Water Act as amended by section 401 of P.L. 107-188, the Public Health Security and Bioterrorism Preparedness and Response Act of 2002.

[118] Testimony of Brad Coffey, Association of Metropolitan Water Agencies, before the House Committee on Energy and Commerce, Subcommittee on Environment and Hazardous Materials, June 12, 2008.

[119] See, for example, American Water Works Association, "AWWA Members Urged to Contact Congress on Chemical Security Bill," and Association of Metropolitan Water Agencies, "Drinking Water Security and Treatment Mandates," *Policy Resolution*, October 2008.

[120] Some agencies oversee both safety and security issues. For example, the U.S. Coast Guard has both safety and security responsibilities for ports.

[121] Testimony of Brad Coffey, Association of Metropolitan Water Agencies, before the House Committee on Energy and Commerce, Subcommittee on Environment and Hazardous Materials, June 12, 2008.

---

wish to consider whether the regulated entities and the customers they serve should bear these costs, as is done for other regulated chemical facilities, or by the taxpayers in general through financial assistance to the regulated entities. Additionally, if inclusion of other facility types significantly increases the number of regulated entities, the regulating agency may require additional funds to process regulatory submissions and perform required inspections.

Harmonize Regulations

Other security provisions, such as MTSA, apply to some facilities exempt from the existing chemical facility security regulations. The DHS supports modifying the existing exemption for MTSA facilities to increase security at these facilities to the CFATS standard and modifying the existing exemption for facilities regulated by the Nuclear Regulatory Commission to clarify the scope of the exemption.[122] The EPA has testified that the Obama Administration believes that DHS should be responsible for ensuring consistency of high-risk chemical facility security across all critical infrastructure sectors.[123] If Congress modifies these exemptions, conflicts may arise between requirements under chemical facility security regulations and these other provisions. One approach to resolving these conflicts is to identify which statute would supersede the others, providing a single statutory requirement. Critics of such an approach might assert that the superseding statute does not contain all of the protections present in the other statutes. Another approach might be to require agencies to generally harmonize the regulations implementing each statute. Regulatory agencies might identify and determine the best ways to meet statutory requirements while also limiting regulatory duplication or contradiction.

Such harmonization might reduce the regulatory burden on companies possessing facilities regulated under two frameworks, such as MTSA and CFATS, by allowing a single security approach to the regulations. For example, equivalent credentialing of workers under both regulatory frameworks might limit the regulatory cost of compliance, in contrast to requiring two distinct security credentials. The DHS has established a joint NPPD/U.S. Coast Guard (USCG) working group to evaluate and, where appropriate, implement methods to harmonize the CFATS and MTSA regulations.[124] In contrast, if the process of harmonization leads to a significant increase in security requirements, the regulatory burden faced by industry might also increase.

Congress previously expressed its expectation that DHS would execute a Memorandum of Agreement between NPPD and USCG regarding harmonization of chemical security responsibilities under CFATS and MTSA no later than March 30, 2012.[125] The DHS did not meet this expectation. The Senate Committee on Appropriations, in the report accompanying S. 3216, Department of Homeland Security Appropriations Bill, 2013, directs the DHS Deputy Secretary to continue to report on efforts to harmonize chemical security responsibilities.[126] The report accompanying H.R. 5855, Department of Homeland Security Appropriations Bill, 2013, cites the

---

[122] Testimony of Rand Beers, Under Secretary, National Protection and Programs Directorate, Department of Homeland Security, before the Senate Committee on Homeland Security and Governmental Affairs, March 3, 2010.

[123] Testimony of Peter S. Silva, Assistant Administrator for Water, Environmental Protection Agency, before the Senate Committee on Homeland Security and Governmental Affairs, March 3, 2010.

[124] Testimony of Rand Beers, Under Secretary, National Protection and Programs Directorate, Department of Homeland Security, before the House Committee on Energy and Commerce, Subcommittee on Environment and the Economy, March 31, 2011.

[125] H.Rept. 112-331, p. 947.

[126] S.Rept. 112-169, accompanying S. 3216, Department of Homeland Security Appropriations Bill, 2013, p. 99.

comparative success the U.S. Coast Guard has experienced in implementing facility security regulations compared with NPPD. The House committee directs NPPD, in conjunction with the U.S. Coast Guard, to critically review CFATS implementation and report to the committee on a wide range of specified topics.[127]

Consider Inherently Safer Technologies

Congressional policymakers may choose to address the issue of inherently safer technologies, sometimes called methods to reduce the consequences of terrorist attack. The current statute bars DHS from mandating the presence of absence of a particular security measure. Therefore, DHS cannot require a regulated facility to adopt or consider inherently safer technologies.[128] Congress could choose to continue the current policy or provide DHS with statutory authority regarding inherently safer technologies at regulated chemical facilities. One approach might be to mandate the implementation of inherently safer technologies for a set of processes. Another might be to mandate the consideration of implementation of inherently safer technologies with certain criteria controlling whether implementation is required. A third approach might be to mandate the development of a federal repository of inherently safer technology approaches and consideration of chemical processes against those options listed in the repository. Stakeholders might assess and review the viability of applying these inherently safer approaches at lower cost if such information were centralized and freely available. Alternatively, policymakers might establish an incentive-based structure outside of the chemical facility security mandate to encourage the adoption of inherently safer technologies by regulated entities. Lastly, congressional policymakers might choose to not require any consideration or adoption of inherently safer technology approaches.

The Obama Administration has given some support to the use of inherently safer technologies to enhance security at high-risk chemical facilities. It has established a series of principles directing its policy:

- The Administration supports consistency of inherently safer technology approaches for facilities regardless of sector.

- The Administration believes that all high-risk chemical facilities, Tiers 1-4, should assess [inherently safer technology] methods and report the assessment in the facilities' site security plans. Further, the appropriate regulatory entity should have the authority to require facilities posing the highest degree of risk (Tiers 1 and 2) to implement inherently safer technology methods if such methods demonstrably enhance overall security, are determined to be feasible, and, in the case of water sector facilities, consider public health and environmental requirements.

---

[127] H.Rept. 112-492, accompanying H.R. 5855, Department of Homeland Security Appropriations Bill, 2013, p. 102.

[128] The National Environmental Justice Advisory Council, an EPA advisory committee, has recommended to the EPA that the Administrator use authorities under the Clean Air Act to require chemical facilities to implement inherently safer technology approaches (National Environmental Justice Advisory Council, *Letter to Administrator Jackson*, March 14, 2012). Several congressional policymakers have expressed their opposition to this approach. See, for example, Senator James M. Inhofe, Senator Susan M. Collins, Senator David Vitter, and Senator Mary Landrieu, *Letter to Administrator Jackson*, July 16, 2012; and Representative Fred Upton, Representative Ed Whitfield, and Representative John Shimkus, *Letter to Administrator Jackson*, May 8, 2012.

- The Administration believes that the appropriate regulatory entity should review the inherently safer technology assessment contained in the site security plan for all Tier 3 and Tier 4 facilities. The entity should be authorized to provide recommendations on implementing inherently safer technologies, but it would not have the authority to require facilities to implement the inherently safer technology methods.

- The Administration believes that flexibility and staggered implementation would be required in implementing this new inherently safer technology policy.[129]

A congressional mandate for regulated entities to adopt or consider adopting inherently safer technologies may lead regulated entities to consider factors such as homeland security impact in their chemical process assessments. Some experts assert that existing chemical process safety activities consider and assess inherently safer technology approaches though not necessarily in a homeland security context.[130] These assessments may lead to changes in chemical process when deemed safer, more reliable, and cost-effective. The extent to which homeland security impact has factored into these industry decisions is unknown, but DHS has identified cases where chemical facilities have voluntarily modified chemical processes to lower their CFATS tier. An additional complication to assessing inherently safer technology is the varying amounts and quality of information available regarding industrial implementation of inherently safer technologies. While some facilities have converted to processes generally deemed as inherently safer, other facilities may not have sufficient information available to effectively assess the impacts from changing existing processes to ones considered inherently safer.[131] The differences that exist among chemical facilities, in terms of chemical process, facility layout, and ability to finance implementation, may challenge mandatory implementation of inherently safer technologies at regulated entities. Finally, the National Academies have identified that the chemical industry lacks a common understanding and set of practice protocols for identifying safer processes.[132] Therefore, it seems likely that any such mandate will also require accompanying outreach and educational activities for regulated entities. Even the mandatory consideration of inherently safer technologies may place a financial burden on some small regulated entities. Congress might limit mandatory measures to those facilities considered by DHS to pose the most risk or might provide such financial assistance to regulated facilities.[133]

---

[129] Testimony of Rand Beers, Under Secretary, National Protection and Programs Directorate, Department of Homeland Security, before the Senate Committee on Homeland Security and Governmental Affairs, March 3, 2010.

[130] See, for example, testimony of Dennis C. Hendershot, Staff Consultant, Center for Chemical Process Safety, American Institute of Chemical Engineers, before the Senate Committee on Environment and Public Works, June 21, 2006, S.Hrg. 109-1044.

[131] The DHS Science and Technology (S&T) Directorate is engaged in a Chemical Infrastructure Risk Assessment Project that, among other goals, will assess the potential for safer alternative processes that may reduce risk to a select subset of high volume toxic chemicals (Department of Homeland Security, *FY2010 Budget Justification*, pp. S&T R&D - 27–28). The Chemical Security Analysis Center of the DHS S&T Directorate contracted with the Center for Chemical Process Safety of the American Institute of Chemical Engineers to develop a technically based definition for inherently safer technology. See Center for Chemical Process Safety, American Institute of Chemical Engineers, *Final Report: Definition for Inherently Safer Technology in Production, Transportation, Storage, and Use*, July 2010. The DHS has not adopted the S&T Directorate work as a regulatory definition. Congress has directed DHS to detail and report to Congress the Department's definition of inherently safer technology as it relates to chemical facilities under the purview of CFATS. See H.Rept. 112-331, p. 986.

[132] Committee on Inherently Safer Chemical Processes, National Research Council, *The Use of Methyl Isocyanate (MIC) at Bayer CropScience*, 2012.

[133] Section 401 of the Public Health Security and Bioterrorism Preparedness and Response Act of 2002 (P.L. 107-188) mandated drinking water facilities serving more than 3,300 individuals develop an emergency response plan and (continued...)

Policymakers might choose to try to further incentivize regulated entities to adopt inherently safer technologies. Under the CFATS regulations, facilities that adopt inherently safer technologies might change their assigned risk tier by reducing the amount of chemicals of interest on hand. As of July 2012, more than 2,730 facilities had removed or reduced the amount of chemical of interest stored onsite in order to no longer qualify as a high-risk facility.[134] Policymakers might provide regulated entities that adopt inherently safer technologies with financial or regulatory incentives. Alternatively, policymakers might direct DHS or another agency to perform inherently safer technology assessments for regulated entities, transferring the cost of such assessment from the facility to the federal government.[135] The regulated entity or the overseeing agency might use the results of these assessments to guide implementation.

Modify Information Security Provisions

Congressional policymakers might choose to increase transparency in the CFATS process by altering the information security provisions of the program. Such an approach might include increasing the number and type of individuals granted access to CVI, improving information exchange with first responders, and adjusting the manner by which courts and administrative proceedings handle CVI. The Obama Administration has testified that CVI is a distinct information protection regime and expressed support for maintaining CVI in its current form.[136]

Congress might choose to amend the existing statutory authority to address policy concerns. For example, while still maintaining disclosure prohibitions for vulnerability or security related information, congressional policymakers might require that DHS gather and document comments and information. Such input might come from outside groups, worker organizations, or other trade representatives through formal and informal mechanisms or by the solicitation, development, and use of industry best practices. Policymakers might direct DHS to make specific types of information, such as the results of enforcement activities or the approval of successful implementation of a site security plan, more generally available. By mandating the inclusion of such information gathering or the release of specific information, congressional policymakers might facilitate greater cooperation between various stakeholder groups. Conversely, such requirements may raise concerns about the degree of security given to the protected information, since more individuals will participate in its development and analysis, perhaps increasing the ability of malicious persons to use such information for targeting purposes. As more information about the vulnerability assessment and the security process becomes available, the potential that adversaries might combine this disparate information to obtain insight into a security weakness may increase. Congressional policymakers might require that the executive branch or another

---

(...continued)

perform a vulnerability assessment. Funds were authorized to help offset the costs to these facilities.

[134] Infrastructure Security Compliance Division, Office of Infrastructure Protection, National Protection and Programs Directorate, Department of Homeland Security, *Chemical Facility Anti-Terrorism Standards (CFATS) and Ammonium Nitrate Security Regulation Update*, July 31, 2012.

[135] Following investigation into the explosion at the Bayer CropScience facility in Institute, WV, Members of Congress requested that the Chemical Safety Board provide recommendations on the adoption of alternative chemical processes at the chemical facility. Rep. Henry A. Waxman, Sen. John D. Rockefeller IV, Rep. Bart Stupak, and Rep. Edward J. Markey, *Letter to John Bresland*, May 4, 2009, online at http://energycommerce house.gov/Press_111/20090504/bayer.pdf.

[136] Testimony of Rand Beers, Under Secretary, National Protection and Programs Directorate, Department of Homeland Security, before the Senate Committee on Homeland Security and Governmental Affairs, March 3, 2010.

entity identify the threats or vulnerabilities that might accrue from release of a greater amount of chemical facility security information prior to implementing such a policy change.[137]

Congressional policymakers can choose to alter the information protection regime afforded to chemical facility security information by specifically expanding access to first responders. The existing regulation explicitly states that information developed in response to other laws or regulations, such as Emergency Planning and Community Right-to-Know Act, are not protected from disclosure. Enhancing first responder access to such information might minimize perceived barriers to disclosing information during an accident. For example, Congress might mandate that each jurisdiction with a regulated chemical facility contain a first responder designated as a covered individual.

Congressional policymakers also can choose to further limit dissemination of CVI so as to increase barriers to its release if that is a policy goal. Congress might prohibit DHS from sharing such information outside of the federal government or set particular criteria that would allow CVI access to state and local officials. Limiting the number of individuals with access to CVI may make it more difficult for those wishing to do harm to obtain technical or operational security information. Conversely, state and local officials may not support such an approach, as limitations on distribution may also adversely affect emergency response at a regulated facility or inhibit the ability of state and local law enforcement officials to provide targeted protection of particular chemical facility assets.

Policymakers might also choose to address the issue of identifying and marking protected information by mandating review of marked documents. Congressional policymakers might place this responsibility to review and certify marked information on the chemical facility. Alternatively, the federal government might review and certify documents marked CVI on a regular basis. Industry representatives may not support such a requirement due to the additional regulatory burden caused by the review. Additionally, while such review might potentially limit incorrect marking, it may inhibit information reporting by regulated entities to the federal government. Additionally, absent a penalty for incorrect marking, it is unclear how to ensure compliance.

Congressional policymakers may also address concerns raised regarding the ability of concerned individuals to report misdeeds by creating a "whistleblower" reporting mechanism.[138] One approach might be to codify the current mechanism of reporting such concerns to DHS or a similar federal entity, such as an agency Inspector General. Alternatively, Congress can create a more general exemption to the penalties arising from disclosure of protected information for those individuals who report such concerns to federal officials if that is needed to protect whistleblowers. As part of a whistleblower mechanism, policymakers might choose to extend protections against retaliation or other job-related actions to those individuals availing themselves of current or newly established reporting mechanisms.

---

[137] A similar approach was taken with regard to making available chemical facility information submitted to the EPA under the auspices of the Risk Management Program. In this case, Congress directed the President to assess the potential risk of placing this information on the Internet. See Section 3 of Chemical Safety Information, Site Security and Fuels Regulatory Relief Act (P.L. 106-40). See also, Department of Justice, *Assessment of the Increased Risk of Terrorist or Other Criminal Activity Associated with Posting Off-Site Consequence Analysis Information on the Internet*, April 18, 2000.

[138] While DHS has established a "CFATS Tip-Line" where individuals may report security concerns, individuals using the tip-line accrue no special protections.

Preempt State Regulations

The 110th Congress addressed the issue of federal preemption of state chemical facility security statutes and regulations by placing in statute the requirement that federal regulation preempt the state regulation only when an "actual conflict" occurs between them.[139] Congressional policymakers may choose to further limit the cases where federal regulation would preempt state regulation by affirming the right of states to make chemical facility security regulations that are more stringent than federal regulation even if they conflict. Alternatively, policymakers may choose to increase the number of cases where federal regulations preempt those of a state by expanding the types of conflict, beyond "actual," that will lead to preemption.

Congressional Action

The annual appropriations process provides funding for implementation of chemical facility security regulation. The Continuing Appropriations Resolution, 2013 (P.L. 112-175) extends the statutory authority through March 27, 2013, and provides appropriations for CFATS implementation.

Extend the Existing Authority

The current statutory authority expires on March 27, 2013. Congress is considering extending the existing authority through authorization legislation. The Obama Administration has requested an extension of the existing statutory authority in each budget request. For FY2013, it has requested a one-year extension of this authority until October 4, 2013.[140] It requested a one-year extension of the existing statutory authority to October 4, 2011, in the FY2011 budget and a two-year extension to October 4, 2013, in the FY2012 budget.[141] Congress provided a one-year extension in the DHS appropriation act for FY2011 and FY2012.

H.J.Res. 117/P.L. 112-175

H.J.Res. 117/P.L. 112-175, the Continuing Appropriations Resolution, 2013, became law on September 28, 2012. It extended the existing statutory authority to March 27, 2013.

H.R. 901

H.R. 901, the Chemical Facility Anti-Terrorism Security Authorization Act of 2011, was reported as amended by the House Committee on Homeland Security. The act would amend the Homeland Security Act of 2002 with provisions authorizing DHS oversight of chemical facility security. The provisions of H.R. 901 generally match the existing statutory authority. H.R. 901 would also authorize appropriation of $89.9 million annually from FY2012 through FY2018. The statutory

---

[139] P.L. 110-161, the Consolidated Appropriations Act, 2008, Section 534.

[140] Office of Management and Budget, The White House, *Budget of the United States Government, Fiscal Year 2013, Appendix*, p. 597.

[141] Office of Management and Budget, The White House, *Budget of the United States Government, Fiscal Year 2011, Appendix*, p. 574; and Office of Management and Budget, The White House, *Budget of the United States Government, Fiscal Year 2012, Appendix*, p. 553.

authority would expire on September 30, 2018. In addition, the DHS would be required to approve or disapprove of vulnerability assessments and site security plans within 180 days of receipt and provide technical support to regulated entities qualifying as small businesses. The DHS would issue guidance on how alternative background checks would meet in full or in part any background check personnel security requirement. Finally, the DHS would be required to report to select congressional committees regarding its success at meeting the 180 day requirement, efforts to harmonize CFATS and MTSA regulations, and on the number of jobs created or eliminated due to CFATS regulation.

H.R. 901 was also referred to the House Committee on Energy and Commerce to the Subcommittee on Environment and the Economy. The subcommittee has taken no further action on this bill.

H.R. 908

H.R. 908, the Full Implementation of the Chemical Facility Anti-Terrorism Standards Act, was reported as amended by the House Committee on Energy and Commerce. The act would extend the existing statutory authority to October 4, 2018. H.R. 908 would authorize appropriations of $89.92 million for each fiscal year from FY2012 through FY2018. It would allow the Secretary of Homeland Security to accept security background checks conducted for other purposes. Finally, it would also allow holders of Transportation Worker Identification Credential cards access to CFATS-regulated facilities.

H.R. 916

H.R. 916, the Continuing Chemical Facilities Antiterrorism Security Act of 2011, was referred to the House Committee on Energy and Commerce and the House Committee on Homeland Security. The act would extend the existing statutory authority to October 4, 2015. It would also amend the Homeland Security Act of 2002 to direct the Secretary of Homeland Security to establish a voluntary chemical security training program and a voluntary chemical security exercise program. Finally, it would authorize such sums as necessary for these programs.

H.R. 2017/P.L. 112-33

H.R. 2017/P.L. 112-33, the Continuing Appropriations Act, 2012, became law on September 30, 2011. It extended the existing statutory authority to October 4, 2011.

H.R. 2055/P.L. 112-74

H.R. 2055/P.L. 112-74, the Consolidated Appropriations Act, 2012, became law on December 23, 2011. It extended the existing statutory authority to October 4, 2012.

H.R. 5855

H.R. 5855, the Department of Homeland Security Appropriations Bill, 2013, was passed by the House of Representatives on June 7, 2012. H.R. 5855 would extend the existing statutory authority to October 4, 2013.

S. 473

S. 473, the Continuing Chemical Facilities Antiterrorism Security Act of 2011, was reported with an amendment by the Senate Committee on Homeland Security and Governmental Affairs. S. 473 would extend the existing statutory authority to October 4, 2014. In addition, it would amend the Homeland Security Act of 2002 to direct the Secretary of Homeland Security to establish a voluntary chemical security training program, a voluntary chemical security exercise program, a voluntary technical assistance program, and a chemical facility security advisory board. S. 473 would authorize such sums as necessary for the programs and board.

S. 3216

S. 3216, the Department of Homeland Security Appropriations Bill, 2013, was reported by the Senate Committee on Appropriations. S. 3216 would extend the existing statutory authority to October 4, 2013.

Modify the Existing Authority

Legislation has been introduced in both chambers that would modify the existing authority.

H.R. 225

H.R. 225, the Chemical Facility Security Improvement Act of 2011, was referred to the House Committee on Energy and Commerce and the House Committee on Homeland Security. The act would prohibit the Secretary of Homeland Security from approving a chemical facility site security plan if the plan did not meet or exceed existing state or local security requirements. It would allow the Secretary of Homeland Security to mandate the use of specific security measures in site security plans. The bill would also cause CVI to be treated as sensitive security information in both general and legal proceedings. Finally, the act would no longer prohibit third-party individuals from bringing suit in court to require the Secretary of Homeland Security to enforce chemical facility security regulations against a chemical facility.

H.R. 2890

H.R. 2890 was referred to the House Committee on Energy and Commerce and the House Committee on Transportation and Infrastructure. The act would expand chemical facility security regulation to include public water systems and wastewater treatment facilities and direct the President to delegate such regulatory authority from the Secretary of Homeland Security to the EPA Administrator.

S. 709

S. 709, the Secure Chemical Facilities Act, was referred to the Senate Committee on Homeland Security and Governmental Affairs. The act would codify aspects of the CFATS regulation. It would require facilities to evaluate whether the facility could reduce the consequences of an attack by using a safer chemical or process. The act would authorize DHS to require implementation of those safer measures if a facility has been classified as one of the highest-risk facilities, implementation of safer measures is feasible, and implementation would not increase risk overall by shifting risk to another location. Among other provisions, S. 709 also would increase the participation of employees and employee representatives in developing security plans. S. 709 would alter the current information control regime, aligning it with that for sensitive security information. Finally, S. 709 would allow third-party individuals to file suit against the Secretary of Homeland Security or submit a petition to the Secretary to enforce compliance with statute.

S. 711

S. 711, the Secure Water Facilities Act, was referred to the Senate Committee on Environment and Public Works. The act would authorize the EPA Administrator to regulate community water systems and wastewater treatment facilities for security purposes. S. 711 also would authorize implementation of methods to reduce the consequences of a chemical release from an intentional act. Among other provisions, the Administrator would be directed to promulgate regulations as necessary to prohibit the unauthorized disclosure of controlled information. S. 711 would authorize the Administrator to provide grants or enter into cooperative agreements with states or regulated entities to assist in regulatory compliance.

Author Contact Information

Dana A. Shea
Specialist in Science and Technology Policy
dshea@crs.loc.gov, 7-6844